ᴎᴊᕼᴛ

# SWALEDA
# THE SPIRIT SPE

CU00694363

# Book 2
# FEATURING HEALAUGH
# AND REETH, BUT INCLUDING
# ARKENGARTHDALE AND FREMINGTON
and History for all Swaledale

# by Sandra K. Wood

Published by Corporate Link, Swale View, Low Row, Richmond, North Yorkshire DL11 6NE.

Copyright © Sandra K. Wood, 1990

ISBN No. 0 9512626 2·9

Phototypeset and Printed by
The Parkgate Press Limited, Print House, Borough Road, Darlington, Co. Durham DL1 1SW

Other books by the author: 'KNIGHT'S ERRAND', the biography of Atkinson Grimshaw, artist,
published by Corporate Link 1987.

# ACKNOWLEDGEMENTS

Book II's text provides a backcloth, from which the heritage of all these Dales comes forward. The map on page 14 contains many of the names which are part of this heritage.

May these words speak for themselves and be digested with contemplative pleasure. Each book of this series will have no more than 119 pages, in an attempt to make each book cost-effective, but informative. My hardest task involves what to omit from each book that would be better placed because of other connections in another book!

It cannot be emphasized too strongly that each book in this series is a continuation or clarification of information arising in previous books. There is a very large story here; I can only trust that I may be worthy of presenting it in a fashion that respectfully pays tribute to all those who have contributed to the 'corpus of dale literature', so aptly put recently by one of these writers.

Points of reference for Book II are: A History of Richmond and Swaledale (R. Fieldhouse, B. Jennings, Phillimore); Early Yorkshire Families (Record Series Vol. CXXXV, 1973, The Yorkshire Archaeological Society); Documents Relating to the Swaledale Estates of Lord Wharton in the 16th & 17th Centuries (Arthur Raistrick, M.Y. Ashcroft, N. Yorks. Co. Record Office Publications No. 36); Bulmer's History Directory of N. Yorks., 1890; A History of the Manor and Lead Mines of Arkengarthdale Yorkshire (Leslie Owen Tyson, British Mining Series No. 29); A History of Westmorland (Richard S. Ferguson, Elliot Stock, London); Yesterday our Ancestry (Leonard Webster Pratt, 1929, Christopher Pratt & Sons, Bradford); The Whartons of Wharton Hall (Edward Ross Wharton, 1898, Henry Frowde, London); Chancellor's Ancient Sepulchral Monuments of Essex; LDS Library, Salt Lake City Utah; Calendars of the Patent Rolls - Vol.1., Univ. of Wyoming Library; Will of John Wiseman; Various Harleian Society Books, (LDS Library, Salt Lake City); Calendar of Patent Rolls 2 Eliz. I; Victoria County History, North Riding; The Alderson Family History Society; The Metcalfe Family History Society; Royal County of Berkshire Library and Information Service, Reading Berks; Victoria History of the County of Berks., Vol III; Visitation of Berkshire, 1532, by Thomas Benolte; Visitation of Berkshire, 1623, by Ashmole for Bysshe; Visitation of Berkshire, 1623, by Chitting and Philipott for Camden; (It was also very interesting to see Visitation of Berks., 1665-66, by Ashmole for Bysshe, listing Peacock of Cowley, Co. Berks., arms granted 27 June 1640, naming Robert Peacock, Lord Mayor of Yorke, descending to Wm., Co. Lincoln, Richard, same, to Wm., Jn., of Chawley, Co. Berks., to Jn., same, and Francis (m. Frances, dtr. to Edw: Helyn of Minster Lovell, Co. Oxon.), to Jn., Edwd., Francis, Charles, Wm., Thomas, Rbt., Samuell, Rchd.); and the richest reference source of all, the families who have inherited this past.

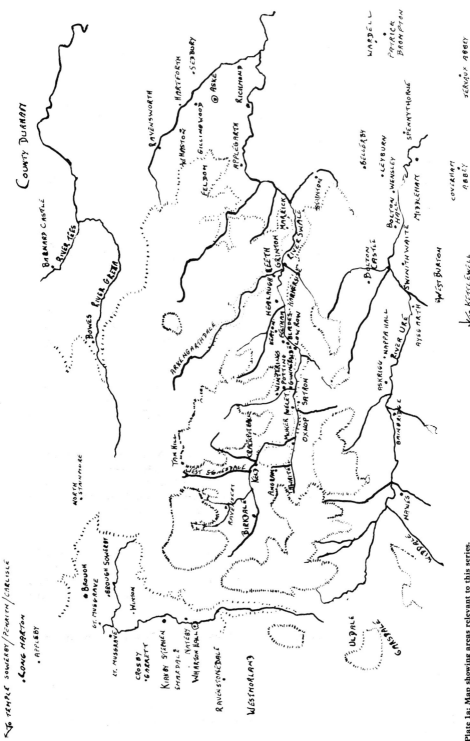

**Plate 1a: Map showing areas relevant to this series.**

# SWALEDALE THE SPIRIT SPEAKS LOUD - BOOK II

As the land in these Dales speaks of its past, may the surviving caretakers of these priceless parcels of history ensure, through their children and other successors, the perpetuity of this rich heritage.

Some years may pass before sufficient funds arise for archaeologists to comment fully on what this series will say, but I would encourage wealthy landowners to consider their even greater riches beneath the soil. Heritage is the only thing in life which cannot be taken away in these progressive times, eroded yes, sunk deeper perhaps. It is the only point at which we can truly value how life has evolved, the only real measure.

Book II opens at Healaugh, where, during the reign of King Stephen (1135-1154), this manor (sometimes known as the manor of Swaledale or of Reeth) was given to Walter de Gaunt, following his marriage to Maud, Stephen's daughter. Stephen was a favourite of Henry I (1100-35), his uncle (buried at Reading Abbey in Berkshire).

When William I (the Conqueror, 1066-87) died, Normandy was left to his eldest son, Robert, and England to William II (called Rufus, 1087-1100), who took over many church estates after forcing Anselm, Archbishop of Canterbury, into exile, 1097. This was the year after Robert went on the 1st Crusade, having pawned Normandy to William II. Henry I was crowned within 3 days of William II's crossbow 'accident' in the New Forest (Hants.).

The subsequent era marks the first traces of England's judicial system and civil service. A power struggle began with the church, also civil war ending with the Treaty of Westminster, through which Stephen finally accepted Henry, Matilda's son, grandson to Henry I, as his adopted son and heir.

Henry II (1154-89) attempted to restore control over the barons and the Church. He exercised overlordship of Wales and Scotland, turning Crown attention for the first time towards Ireland. His eldest surviving son, Richard I (the Lionheart, 1189-99), spent a large part of his reign in the Crusade against the Saracens (led by Saladin) in the Holy Land. Joining the siege of Acre, after capturing Cyprus, he then triumphantly marched on Jerusalem, achieving only a truce with Saladin, 1192.

Having lost rule over Normandy to King Philip of France, 1204, John (1199-1216), Henry II's youngest son, taxed English barons heavily to subsidize recovery of French territory. Returning, unsuccessfully, from France in 1214, confrontation with the rebellious barons at Runnymede resulted in the Magna Carta, 1215, asserting protection of all men by the law, with no man being above it. Civil war started 1216 when John reneged on this charter.

With London occupied by Prince Louis of France, Henry III (1216-72), John's eldest son, ended this war through the Treaty of Kingston, 1217. Henry III was made sovereign over Normandy by the Treaty of Paris, 1259, having married Eleanor, sister of the Queen of France, in 1236.

Returning from the Crusade in 1274, Edward I (1272-1307) had been King for two years, having left before his father's burial in Westminster Abbey, 1272. His five years of government administration, before departing for the Crusade, resulted in law reforms that led to the Model Parliament of 1295.

Having married twice (Eleanor of Castile and Margaret of France) and before a third attempt to subdue Scotland, Edward's eldest son, Edward II (1307-27) succeeded him. He was defeated by the Scots under Robert the Bruce at Bannockburn, 1314. Influence over him was attempted by the Earl of Leicester and the Despenser family, whose interference led to his Queen, Isabella, rebelling against him in 1326.

Edward III (1327-77) succeeded against the Scots, 1333, and later took on France, claiming to be the rightful heir to the French crown through his mother. This resulted in the Hundred Years War (1337-1453) with France. During his reign the Black Death devastated England 1348-50, followed by other epidemics 1361-2, 1369 and between 1374-1474 in this part of the world which affected the North Yorkshire economy, depending heavily on mills and sheep farming for wool trade. Reduction in population and useable land, resulting from Scottish invasions and epidemics, led to drastically reduced revenues.

When Edward III's heir, Richard II (1377-99), son of Edward, the Black Prince, was crowned, aged 10, the Parliamentary Council was led by Richard's loyal uncle, John of Gaunt. As a result of the peasants' revolt against high taxes in 1381, the 'Merciless Parliament', led by the Duke of Gloucester, executed many as traitors in 1388, previously supported by Richard when their leader, Wat Tyler, was killed.

Henry Bolingbroke, Richard's cousin and son of John of Gaunt, revolted and captured Richard at Conway Castle in 1399. The king was imprisoned at Pontefract Castle and probably murdered later. Grandson of Edward III, Henry had been exiled by Richard II for his part in the 'Merciless Parliament' and forced him now to abdicate the Crown. Richard II had confiscated John of Gaunt's estates. Until 1408, there was much plotting and many uprisings against this Henry IV (1399-1413). He empowered the Church to burn heretics.

Archbishop of Arundel and Henry, The Prince of Wales, handled the affairs of State from 1406; Henry IV was ill. Archbishop Arundel led the Council, in deference to Henry IV's wishes. Henry V (1413-22) did succeed, though, also at Agincourt, 1415, and Rouen, recognised as the heir to the French Crown, 1420, at the Treaty of Troyes.

Having married Catherine, the daughter of Charles VI of France, Henry died, as well as the French King. Henry VI (1422-61, deposed, 1470-71) was king before his first birthday. Charles VII was crowned, 1429, at Rheims and Henry also was crowned as King of France at Paris, 1431, devoutly opposed to war over France as the Hundred Years War was nearing an end.

The Duke of York was appointed Protector in 1454 (Henry VI declared insane), claiming the Throne himself, 1455; he was killed at the Battle of Wakefield 1460. Edward IV (1461-70, 1471-83), York's son, was crowned in 1461, continuing the Wars of the Roses which began in 1455.

Henry VI fled, taken to the Tower 1465, reinstated 1470, but was murdered in 1471 when Edward returned from exile (following Lancastrian opposition and withdrawal of support from the Earl of Warwick, 1470). Edward died, 1483, before his second invasion of France.

From Edward III, along with Edward the Black Prince to John of Gaunt, had also descended Edmund of Langley to Richard of Conisburgh to Richard, Duke of York, to Edward IV and Richard III (1483-85).

Edward IV's will provided that his brother, Richard, Duke of Gloucester, would be Protector of Edward V (1483), 12, and his brother Richard, 9, whose mother Elizabeth Woodville (formerly widow of prominent Lancastrian, Sir John Grey) placed them in the care of a Regency Council.

Through Richard's deception, the boys disappeared, after an interim period in the Tower. Richard's allies came to London from Yorkshire; he received theological support that Edward IV's marriage was invalid, resulting in Parliament asking Richard to take the Crown.

In opposition, Elizabeth Woodville married off her daughter, Elizabeth of York, to Henry Tudor, exiled Lancastrian heir. This united the Houses of York and Lancaster and ended the Wars of the Roses. Henry VII (1485-1509) was the son of Edmund Tudor and Margaret Beaufort and grandson of Catherine, Henry V's widow, who later married Owen Tudor.

Henry VIII (1509-47) was Duke of York before being crowned and Henry VII was Earl of Richmond (Yorks.) before being crowned 1485. Richmond Palace was renamed from the Palace of Sheen when Henry VII was crowned.

Appertaining to the Richmondshire Alderson family, when King Henry VII died, aged 52, at Richmond Palace, 21st April, 1509, at his funeral in Westminster Abbey was William Alderson, one of the eleven 'children of the chapel' present. William Alderson was also one of the ten 'children' present in the King's Chapel for the coronation of Henry VIII and Catherine of Aragon (they married 11th June).

For William Alderson and Arthur Lovekyn, referred to as 'our scholars', was an order from Henry VIII at the Palace of Richmond, 20th November, 1511, for a 'warrant to the Great Wardrobe' to provide them with gowns of tawney cloth, etc. Exchequer accounts of Sir Andrew Wyndesore, keeper of the Great Wardrobe at that time, gives details of dates of 75 such warrants, including 14th December, 1511, for the above.

It was suggested that funerals were a matter for priests and monks and William could possibly have been a chorister. State papers (Domestic, Henry VIII, 1509-11) describe William as a 'King's Scholar'.

It is also important to mention here that Henry VI's wife was Margaret of Anjou. She led his army during the civil war following the Duke of York's claim to the Throne, 1455. Her son, Edward, Henry's heir, was killed at the Battle of Tewkesbury, 1471. Edmund Beaufort, Duke of Somerset, assisted her in opposing Richard, Duke of York. After a victory at Northampton, Margaret had control of the government from 1456-60.

Margaret descended of the House of Lorraine and Guise from Rene le Bon, duc of Anjou (also titular King of Naples and Sicily). He married Isabella, Duchesse of Lorraine. From Rene, after several generations, descended Claude of Lorraine, 1st duc de Guise (1496-1550), whose daughter, Mary of Guise, married James V of Scotland, becoming parents of Mary Queen of Scots.

Claude's sons, Francois de Lorraine, 2nd duc de Guise (1519-63), and Charles de Guise, Cardinal of Lorraine, (c.1525-74), controlled the French government in the reign of Francis II (the first husband of Mary, Queen of Scots, who was held prisoner at Bolton Castle, Wensleydale). They defended the Roman Catholic cause and that against the Protestant Huguenots.

Francois's son, Henri de Lorraine, 3rd duc de Guise (1550-88), helped to plan the massacre of Huguenots on Saint Bartholomew's Day, 1572. Certain branches of the Richmondshire Place family, whose photos are within, maintain that members of this family came to England as a result of this Huguenot persecution.

Henry VII (1485-1509) had effected a peace treaty with Scotland 1499, followed by the marriage of his daughter to James IV of Scotland. English rule in Ireland was also consolidated, 1494, with conquest still proving too expensive in Henry VIII's reign. War with Scotland began again in 1542, during Henry VIII's (1509-47) reign. Gradual moves towards Protestantism were evident towards the end of that reign, after the dissolution of the monasteries 1536-39.

From Henry VIII's wives came: Edward VI (1547-53) of Jane Seymour (wife 3); Mary I (1553-58) of Catherine of Aragon (1); Elizabeth I (1558-1603) of Anne Boleyn (2). Other wives: Anne of Cleves (4); Catherine Howard (5); Catherine Parr (6). Mary I married Philip of Spain.

It is interesting to note here that Philip, third Lord Wharton, born 1555, was named after his God-father, King Philip of Spain. Of his two sons, Sir George and Sir Thomas, the latter and youngest lived at Aske near Richmond (1587-1622). He married Lady Philadelphia, only daughter of Sir Robert Carey, Earl of Monmouth, and granddaughter of Henry Lord Hunsdon, first cousin (through his mother, Mary Boleyn) to Queen Elizabeth I. They are buried together at Easby, near Richmond.

Of this Sir Thomas's two sons are Philip, later 4th Lord Wharton (1613-96), and Sir Thomas Wharton (1615-84). Philip, the Good Lord Wharton, met Charles II, May 29th 1660, accompanying him from Greenwich to London, and also attended his coronation, April 23rd 1661, later receiving King William III at Wooburn (Bucks.). In 1692, Philip, Lord Wharton, conveyed lands near Healaugh to trustees for 1050 bibles to be given yearly in certain towns and villages of the four counties where his estates were: Buckinghamshire, Yorkshire, Westmorland and Cumberland. He died at Hampstead and was buried at Wooburn.

Also fascinating to note is that the Hunsdon and Carey names appear on the pedigree for Reading's Knollys (pronounced 'Noles') family in Berkshire when Catherine Carey, first cousin to Queen Elizabeth I, married Sir Francis Knollys. King Henry VIII granted Sir Francis the estate of Rotherfield Greys, north of Henley (Oxon.) to which were later added the manors of Caversham and Cholsey.

Sir Francis was abroad during Queen Mary's reign. His wife's mother was sister to Anne Boleyn. Treasurer of Queen Elizabeth's Royal Household, Sir Francis also had Mary Queen of Scots in his charge at Carlisle and took her to Bolton. He taught her English and attempted to convert her from Catholicism to Protestantism.

Sir Francis entertained Queen Elizabeth I at Reading Abbey in 1572, where she was later resident in 1601. His daughter, Lettice, set a memorial to her first husband, the Earl of Leicester, in Beauchamp Chapel, Warwick. Her brother, William, created Lord Banbury by Charles I in 1626, died 1632. Knighted by Leicester, the Queen sent Sir Francis in 1585 to James VI of Scotland with a message of no support.

When William's first wife died in 1628, he married Elizabeth Howard, daughter of Thomas, Earl of Suffolk, who later married Edward, fourth Lord Vaux. Elizabeth's sister, Frances, then Countess of Essex, married Rochester (Robert Carr), Earl of Somerset. The King, for some guilty offence, pardoned the Somersets, conditionally, that they remain prisoners at either of Lord Knollys's houses of Greys and Caversham.

Greys Castle dates from the reign of King John, 13th c., built by an Archbishop of York, Walter de Grey, for his nephew, John, one of the original Knights of the Garter. This estate passed from the Greys after 1387 to the Lovells, then to the Crown on the attainder of Francis 9th Baron Lovell, and ultimately to Sir Francis Knollys. His 6th son, also Sir Francis, had a daughter Lettice, who married Sir Thomas Vachell, from whom the Whartons purchased the Manor of Healaugh.

In 1633, Sir Thomas Vachell, Knight, was a customary tenant of Healaugh, along with Jeffrey and George Lonsdale, Symon Wilson, John Langstaffe, John (by his uncle), James and John (the elder) Gallaway, Edward Hodgson, James and Ralfe Robinson, William Arrondell, Thomas Kipling (an infant) and Thomas Waller.

Using spellings as seen, Sir Thomas Vachell was listed as a 'freeholder which does suite of courte', knight out of Crakpott, along with Christopher Haggston and Edmond Clarkson, all bracketed together with the marginal note -Wycliffe. Also listed: the heires of Margaret Siningthwaite, marginal note - the king's tenants of Crakpot; Salamon Swaile; John and Bygon Blades; Richard Hutchinson for the Haver Flatt and the North Feild, Charles Hutchinson and Marke Close for the Common feild and every third rent ob' and nyne pence 67 yeare, all bracketed with marginal note - Franck's land; Richard Jefferson, Mathew Harrison, Richard Fothergill, marginal note - Curland; James Milner senior of Crackpott, marginal note - Thursby; Jeffray Douglas in lease,for (two thousand crossed out) and payes onely suite of courte and rent; William Arrondell in fee farm and doth suite of courte and payes rent; John Hutchinson, free rent at Ruckroft, marginal note - Tempest land, also Richard junior, Robert, Leonard Hutchinson and James Alderson of the same.

For further insight, 'freeholders of improvements of Rawe' were; Leonard Hutchinson, West Intacke; Roger Alderson; the heires of Richard Alderson; Robert, Richard younger, John, Richard, Michael and Richard the elder Hutchinson; Richard Hutchinson for the said Johns, marginal note - Thursby; Christopher, Matthew Alderson; Christopher Haggett; Francis Jefferson, same note as Jefferson 'freeholder' above and also note - Franck's land; and John Metcalfe. All these were to be paid upon Sunday after Mary Magdalin day and Sunday after St. Andrew day by equall porcions. All earlier bracketed and marginally noted - Wycliffe - were for the lease rent of West Stonesdale due at St. Andrew day onely.

Deeds dated February, 1560, relating to the purchase of a moiety (½) of the Manor of Healaugh by Lord Wharton from Sir Thomas Vachell in 1635 include: a grant for (1) John Flower of Whitwell, Co. Rutland (2) John Molyneux of Thorpe, Co. Notts. for: all his part of the manor of 'Helowe' in Swaledale with appurtenances in Healaugh, Grinton and Swaledale including coal mines, lead mines and 'loott ure', warrented to be of the clear yearly value of £23;

also, dated June, 1561, exemplification of fine at Westminster in Trinity term 3 Elizabeth, John Molyneux, plaintiff, John Flower, deforciant, fourth part of manor of 'Heloo in Swaledale' with appurtenances, half part of 60 messuages, 30 cottages, 80 tofts, fourth part of one water mill, 40 gardens, 40 orchards, 1000 acres of land, 600 acres meadow, 2000 acres pasture, 600 acres wood, 8000 acres moor, 6000 acres moss, 4000 acres turbary, 8000 acres furze and heath and £5 worth of rents with appurtenants in 'Heloo, Gronton, and Swaldale', also free fishing in water of Swale in Healaugh, Grinton and Swaledale and free chase in Healaugh, Swaledale and Grinton;

also, dated March, 1620, a mortgage between (1) Gregory Smith of London, merchant, and John Haulsey of London, (2) Sir Thomas Vachell of Coley, Co. Berks. moiety of the moiety of the manors of 'Healaughe and Swaldale and Swaindale in Swauldale' and moiety of all messuages, houses, edifices, buildings, cottages, barns, stables, orchards, gardens, mills, lands, tenements, meadows, closes, feeding pastures, commons, woods, underwoods, lead mines, coal mines and other mines whatsoever, waters, warrens, fishings, wastes grounds, moors, marshes, chases, wards, marriages, reliefs, escheats, fines, heriots, courts, courts leet, view of frank pledge, rents of free and customary tenements etc., and all moiety of all manors, messuages, cottages, lands, etc. heretofore bargained and sold by Sir John Mollineux of Thorpe, Co. Notts. to Thomas Meade of Stansteed Mountfitchett, Co. Essex, gent, Thomas Woodcock, citizen and grocer of London now deceased, and Gregory Smith of London, merchant, in the several towns, parishes, hamlets or fields of Healaugh, Swauldale and Grinton or within 20 miles of same;

also, dated March 1620, a schedule of bond debts annexed in connection with a mortgage to secure payments in discharge of bonds (1) Gregory Smith and John Haulsey of London (2) Sir Thomas Vachell of Coley, Co. Berks., naming William Courten of London, merchant, on 8th Oct. next, payable at house of William Rolfe, serivener, in Fleet Street, John Van Vadock, merchant, on 12 Nov. 1621, payable at the shop of Lawrence Newman, serivener, in the parish of St. Michael in Cornhill, Henry Tweedy, esq., on 15 Nov. next, payable at the house of said Henry Tweedy in Austin Fryers, William Middleton gent, payable at the shop of Mr. Morgan in Fleet Street, William Ingram gent, payable at the shop of Mr. Morgan, both previous on 27 Oct. 1621, John Latche of the Strand gent, on 18 Nov. 1621, payable at the house of William Clifton, serivener, in Fleet Street, Sir Richard Younge, Knight, on 12 Nov. next, payable at his house in Aldermanbury, Thomas Plomer, merchant, payable at his house in St. Lawrence, Powltneys Lane., William Rodway, merchant tailor, payable at his house at Bassinghall, both previous on 19 Nov. 1621, Anthony Thaire, leatherseller, payable at his house in Pettycoate Lane, Agnes Heydon, widow, payable at her shop or warehouse in Milk Street, John Vachell gent, payable at the font stone in the Temple Church near Fleet Street, three previous on 21 Nov. 1621;

also, dated July 1628, a conveyance (1) Thomas Meade of Stannsteed Mountfitchett, Co. Essex gent (2) Sir Thomas Vachell of Coley, Berks. for property as above together with moiety of lands and tenements called Parradice and Foelinges with appurtenances in Swaledale sometime in the occupation of Anthony Brackenbury, sometime parcel of possessions of late monastery of Mount Grace.

One of the lease schedules, dated 20 June 1635, attached to a deed convenant between (1) Sir Thomas Vachell of Coley, Berkshire, Knight, and Tanfield Vachell of Coley, son of John Vachell of Warfield, Berks. (2) Philip Lord Wharton and his wife Lady Elizabeth was witnessed and signed, among others, by a Richard Browne.

From a 1561 survey of Lord Wharton's estates in the north of England were included free tenants of the manor of Healaughe in Swawdaile: the heirs of Sir Ralph Bulmer, knight (the same heirs holding lands/tenements of Rowcrofte); Marmaduke Francke of Bretton, esq; Christofer Currell, lands and tenements of Rethe; John Swalle, manor of West Grynton; William Thursbye, John Wycliffe and heirs of Margaret Swynnyngthwate, all holding lands/tenements Crakepott.

Tenants listed for the township of Healaughe of that manor and forest were: Simon, Anthony, Stephen Arrundell; John Plaice; John Dent; Gabriell Metcalfe; George and the wife of Ralph Close; Simon Robinson; John Symsonn; William Mylner; Ralph and James Galawaye.

For Reithe: Geoffrey Garth (also including ¼ of a corn mill); John Close (holding remaining ¾ mill); Anthony Parkynn, John Symsonn and Jenet Atkinson (lately occupied by Michael Atkinson); Mathew Metcalfe (Gressum laid on G. Atkinson); Thomas Cowplannd's wife; Geoffrey Charder; Thomas Abroe, clerk; James Coott'; George Atkinson (whose Gressum mentions a separate one for Chappell Close); Robert Hirde, John Robinsonn and wife of Geoffrey Charder; Ralph Playce; James Typladye's wife.

Kearton: William and George Carter and James' wife.

Healaughe Parke: Gabrielle Metcalfe, two houses.

Henry, Lord Scroupe, was tenant of Westonesdal and Christopher Conyers of Marske, esq., at Eaststonsdal. Dame Agnes Musgreve (a Wharton relative) was at Ravenseat along with Edward Dennte, Christopher, John and James Rawe and Richard and Leonard Coote.

Amongst the remaining areas listed were: Brockabank, Blades, Law Rawe, Feetham, Pottinge, Gunnerside, Borwayns, Winteringarths, Satteron, Covethouse, Ulles' and Ivelet. Muker Manor included Oxnoppe, Thwait, Angrame and Birkedaill. These will be included with Book III, and include families of Wensley, Clarkson, Naytbye, Rawe, Freer, Butterfield, Symsonn, Pratt, Blaydes, Scott, Metcalfe, Paycoke, Bradrigge, Keirtonn, Parke-alias Jenkynn, Mylner, Close, Wharton , Alderson, Hudsonn, Arkeye, Cott', Hutchensonn, Shawe, and Wycliffe.

It would appear that, from very early times in Swaledale, the destinies of its people were in the hands of either monasteries, abbeys, etc., supported by powerful persons or favoured persons themselves once the monasteries and last abbeys were dissolved. During that period, Sir Thomas Vachell was granted by the King in 1540 the life-office of supervisor of 'the honours, castles, domains, manors, lands, tenements, and other possessions of the King which had belonged to the Abbey of Reading, also of the possessions once belonging to the priory of Leominster in Hertfordshire'. These were in 13 counties.

The Vachells of Coley and Tilehurst, near Reading, have been quoted as one of the most ancient families in the Royal County of Berkshire, with history traceable as far back as 1240. John Vachell, one of the Knights of the Shire in 1324, was possibly the son of John who in 1297 was appointed one of the commissioners to buy wool in the counties of Oxford and Berkshire.

A Walter Vachell was a juror for the borough of Reading at the assizes of 1261, followed later by John and Roger Vachell. William (d. 1481) was grandfather to the Thomas who was friend and correspondent of Thomas Cromwell.

On this Thomas's death in 1553, the family estates were regranted to his nephew (Walter's son) and heir Sir Thomas Vachell, who was Sheriff of Berkshire in 1610, living at Coley. After he died in 1638, his nephew Tanfield (John's son) became heir. He was member for Reading in the Long Parliament and also Sheriff of Berkshire.

Tanfield Vachell died in 1658 and was buried at St. Mary's Reading. The great grandson of the Sir Thomas of the vast land inheritance married Ann, daughter of William Taileur, alias Danvill, who was surveyor of the works of Windsor Castle.

When the Gaunts were granted Healaugh Manor (Stephen's reign 1135-54) it included all the woodlands, commons and wastes in Fremington, Harkerside and Whitaside, as well as the upper Dale mentioned previously. Robert de Gaunt granted a sub-manor at Fremington to Hervey, Lord of Ravensworth, whose claim probably descended of Bodin, Lord Ravensworth, who held land at Reeth and Grinton when the Domesday Book was made up 1085/6.

In addition to the Forest of Swaledale, the Forest of Arkengarthdale and the New Forest was the second hunting chase (in which the Lords of Richmond, 14th c., employed seven foresters as well as the master forester).

Walter de Gaunt founded the Augustinian Bridlington Priory c. 1113, to which his wife Maude granted St. Andrews at Grinton, including rights to the tithes from the whole manor of Healaugh and of Grinton. After Walter confirmed this c. 1125-30, his granddaughter, Alice, some 40-50 years later, gave the canons pasture rights in Whitaside. They could keep and cultivate the clearances they had made since Walter died 1139. Alice's uncle, Robert de Gaunt, held the manor 1185-91.

25½ acres west of Grinton (previously given by Walter to Ralph Pech) were acquired from Ralph's son William in the early 13th c.. Gilbert de Gaunt (d. 1241) allowed the canons to extend their 'Court of Grenton', adjacent to the churchyard, and build a new house there. Gilbert also gave extensive pasture rights in upper Swaledale, west of Whitsundale Beck, the Swale and Oxnop Gill to the Cistercians of Rievaulx Abbey. These rights were so exclusive as to exclude pasture for local cattle.

Bridlington Priory was allowed by Marrick Priory to grind its malt and corn at the manorial mill, Grinton. Bridlington's corn and meadow was protected by this priory of Roger de Aske (established 1154-8).

A survey of 1273/4 showed that Gilbert de Gaunt had a manor house, 100 acres of arable land, a meadow at Fytun (Feetham) and Skaleflat, with 27½ acres, and a corn mill. Apart from the sub-manor of Fremington with the Ravensworths, William Overswale had land in Grinton and Reeth, these being the only major landholders besides Bridlington Priory. Within the manor of Healaugh, below Arkle Town there were 9 tenants in 'Arkelgarth'.

The Gaunts held Healaugh until 1298, when it was divided between 2 heiresses, during which time a hall, a chapel and stables were built. From above, it is possible to detect visual evidence of this hall near Hall Garth.

Following lawsuits which left the Gaunts with hunting rights only, later surrendered in 1409, Bridlington Priory had effectively, by the 13th century, formed the new 'manor of Grinton'. If the assumption made in 'A History of Richmond and Swaledale' is correct, the major taxpayer in Arkengarthdale around that time was Sir Roger Miniot, a surname similar to a John Miniott who held lands in Carlton Miniott, anciently held by the Barons de Mowbray. Anciently, Thirsk Parish included Thirsk township,Carlton Miniott, Sand Hutton and Sowerby.

Having previously mentioned the moiety of the manors of 'Healaugh and Swaldale and Swaindale in Swauldale', plus having also seen that William Thursbye was a free tenant of the manor of Healaugh, one could become interested in the family of Thoresby, whose descendants ended with FitzHugh of Ravensworth, a family name previously owning a sub-manor of Fremington.

FitzHugh of Ravensworth descended of Bardulf, an illegitimate son of Count Eudo of Penthievre, half brother to Count Alan I (whose descendants held the Honour of Richmond until Henry IV granted it to Ralph Neville, Earl of Westmorland, in 1399). Bardulf received large holdings from Bodin, including Ravensworth and others in Richmondshire. His son, Acaris, succeeded him, a main tenant of Count Stephen 1130. He gave St. Martin's Priory, Richmond, tithes from Ravensworth and elsewhere, also holding 3 1/6 knights' fees, including castle-guard at Richmond, also rendered by his grandson Henry son of Hervey. Acaris played a prominent role in founding Jervaulx Abbey.

Hervey gave Ravensworth land to Marrick Priory, being given the forestership of the New Forest and Arkengarthdale by Earl Conan (Alan's great nephew who built the Richmond Castle's keep, 12th c.) and was succeeded by his son before 1184. From Henry's son Ranulf and Ranulf's grandson, Hugh, son of Henry, descended Henry, son of Hugh of Ravensworth, summoned to Parliament 1321-51. When George, Lord FitzHugh, died 1513, his co-heirs were his aunt, who married Sir John Fenys or Fynes, son of Richard Lord Dacre, and his first cousin, Sir Thomas Parr of Kendal.

It is important to include here that Sir Thomas Parr was Master of the Wards and Comptroller to King Henry VIII, whose daughter Katherine was Henry VIII's 6th wife. He descended through the de Roos family via Elizabeth Roos, an heiress to Peter de Brus de Skelton, who inherited a moiety of the barony of Kendal. In Henry VIII's time, the Richmond fee was a moiety of the barony of Kendal. A moiety is one-half.

Two of Peter de Brus's sisters divided a moiety of the barony of Kendal between them. One married Marmaduke de Thweng a family name which has entered another of the Dales families' histories, to be covered another time. Queen Elizabeth I wound up with both the Richmond (½) and Marquis Fees (¾ of the barony of Kendal). ¼ of the Barony of Kendal passed through the de Thweng family, via marriage ultimately to Henry Bowes Howard, Earl of Berkshire, and afterwards to the Levens family, who had previously been granted it by the Crown from the Duke of Richmond and Somerset. Another time it was sold to the grandson of the same Levens's who had it the first time!

Also interesting is that the Richmond Fee also brought 'customary and dry rents' from Grasmere, Langdale, Loughbrigg, Ambleside, Undermillbeck, Troutbeck, Applethwaite, Fishery and ferry of Windermere, Crosthwaite and Lyth, New Hutton, Casterton, Strickland, Ketel, Heslington, Thornton, Westhouse and Masinghill.

There are two Thoresby areas, one of which is Thoresby, in Carperby, parish of Aysgarth, which was held by Gospatric from Count Alan, along with a manor in Askrigg, parish of Aysgarth, formerly held by Archil. Gospatric inherited land in Ilton, Masham parish.

Archil (b. c. 1020) was son of Ecgfrid. His son Gospatric (b. c. 1050) had two sons, Uctred (b. c. 1075) and Dolfin. Uctred gave Whitby Abbey land in Cayton 1087-1109. Torfin, said to be his son, gave, with his wife Maud de Fribois and Alan his son, her land dowery in Allerston to Rievaulx Abbey. Alan confirmed his father's gift to Whitby Abbey in 1174 of the Church of Crosby Ravensworth, Westmorland. Alan's wife was daughter and heir to Roger Dispenser; their daughter, Helen, married Hugh de Hastings and Robert Vipont. Helen's son, Thomas de Hastings, inherited and descended in the Hastings family.

Gospatric's grandson, Torfin, of Dolfin, was given in a Cottonian roll as father of Peter de Thoresby. Torfin's brother, Swain, was given as the father of Robert de Thoresby , to whom Thoresby passed when his cousin Peter died without issue. Peter, son of Torfin of Askrigg (presumed to be the same as Peter de Thoresby), gave Carperby land to Marrick Priory c. 1174-89.

Torfin's and Swain's brother, another Uctred, was enfeoffed of lands by Roger de Mowbray, and held land in Conistone, Kettlewelldale, Burnsall (both of the honour of Skipton) and Hebden. Privileges in Hebden were given to Fountains Abbey by Uctred's son, Simon, who descended to a granddaughter who married Nicholas of York and had son, William of York (d. 1282), whose son William took the name of Hebden until the 15th century.

Dolfin's son Swain gave Horton in Ribblesdale land to Jervaulx Abbey. Swain's grandson, Richard, of Robert, witnessed a Marrick charter before 1204. In 1286-7 Peter, son of Hugh of Thoresby, held Carperby land of Avice Marmion, who was holding of the Earl of Richmond. Peter held Thoresby land with William, son of Nicholas of York (holding of the steward's fee of the earldom). Hugh held Thoresby in 1316.

From Swain's son, Thomas (witnessed Arncliffe and Threshfield charters 12th c. ), descended Adam de Staveley (gave Calton land to Bolton Priory, all lands of his fee in Ilton, Swinton and Warthermarske, in Swinton, to Fountains Abbey, land in Horton in Ribblesdale to St. Clement's Priory, York - attached to the church given later by daughter Alice, gave all his forest of Lonsdale to William de Mowbray, held Honour of Knaresborough land in Farnham and a knight's fee in Staveley, married Alice, daughter of William de Percy of Kildale, who brought Barwick on Tees in frank-marriage), whose daughter and heir Alice married, 1211, Ranulf, son of Henry of Ravensworth. Alice died 1250-53, her inheritance pasing to the family of FitzHugh of Ravensworth.

Swaledale and Arkengarthdale land testifies to some of the richest and most exciting history in the United Kingdom. Arkengarthdale will be covered in greater depth, historically, and with more photos in later books of this series.

Another family which carries forth much heritage is the Wiseman family, which, among others, relates to families of Brown, Sunter, Ward, Rukin, Cherry, Harker, Hunter, Johnson, Jacques, Blades, Heslop, Ideson, Spence, Birkbeck, Garth, Allen, Raw, Darby, Whaley, Dunn, Slack, White, Simpson, Coates, Tiplady, Stabler, Page, Turnbull, Beadle, Richardson, Alton, Clark, Dolphin, Kay, Bagshaw, Pedley, Milner, Spensley, Miscamble, Robinson, Hird, Cleminson, Fawcet, Alderson, Pratt, Rachford, Cooper, Alsop, Lobley, Blenkiron, Kittoe, Lemke, Jeffers, Peacock, Rowlands, Kitching, Heron, Gaines-Burrill, Brammah, Turnbull, Steele, Smith, Royston and Smithson.

Anne Broderick of Haverdale Bank, 1913, wrote to Mrs. George Brown, Dubbin Garth, Low Row, details of Wiseman relatives, mentioning that Queen Elizabeth sold to Wiseman in 1599, in a certain conveyance, which he resold in about 37 conveyances. She had previously sold Summer Lodge on April 11, 1588 to Edward Downing and Thomas Beste, with other property.

From the Patent Rolls, P.R.O. C66/1505: 'Grant to Richard Wiseman, citizen and Goldsmith of London and a certain Francis Fitche of London, gent, and heirs and assigns of Richard Wiseman in consideration of £1463-9-2. Paid by Richard Wiseman of the Manor of Grinton late belonging to the Monastery and Priory of Bridlington, land called Gresrermes, cottages in Grinton, Premises in Netherwhitton, Overwhitten, Harkerside, Lowespenceley, Haverdell, and Sumerlodge and woods, reserving advowson's and lead with the Manors of Fremington and Grinton to hold as 'of the Honour of Hampton Court', reciting 13 leases of premises in Grinton to various people.'

These lands were on the south side of the Swale, extending from the boundary of Ellerton Manor, below Cogden (east) to Haverdale Beck (west). Robert Wiseman, executor of estate, sold to Rev. Henry Simpson, 1619 (Richard Wiseman d. Nov. 11, 1618), who subsequently sold to Roger Hillary, whose family retained nearly a century.

Richard (c. 1545-1618) married Mary Browne (d. 1635/38, aged 80), whose parents were Robert Browne, City Merchant of London, and Margaret, cousin and heir of Thomas Lucas, London gent.

Richard's parents were John, of Wimbish and Seborewe Hall of Felstead (father John, Northend and Bradocks in Wimbish), and Joane Lucas, whose father was citizen of London. Their children were: Thomas (m. Jane Vaughan); Sir Ralph (m. Elizabeth Barley, Catherine Rich of Horndon); George (m. Martha Strangman of Hadley Castle, Mary Barnadestor); Phillip; this Richard;

Richard; William (m. Elizabeth Jocelyn); John; Anne (m. William Fitch of Lytsell and a Pudsey of Yorkshire and Essex).

Richard's Coat of Arms appears on his elaborate and detailed mural monument in the south wall of the chancel of Willingale Doe Church, Essex, dedicated also to his wife and son, Sir Robert. Families within their Arms are Wiseman, Browne, Tillesworth, Lucas, Hilles, Penne, Brackenbury, Bailliawle and Paynell. Richard and Mary are buried at St. Lawrence Pountney, London. (Several of these family names appear in 'Early Yorkshire Families', Vol. CXXXV, 1973.)

Their children were Sir Robert, Margaret, Richard, Sir Richard (m. Mary Hewyt, Lucy Griffin), Mary (m. George Ward), William, William, Ursula (m. Simon Harvey), Elizabeth (m. Sir William Hewyt), Thomas (m. Elizabeth Backhouse), John and Edward.

Quite remarkably, even in 1910, Swaledale evaluations showed: Fremington - Land, buildings, owner Bellerby Church, occupier Alice, Eliz. Moore, owner Bolton Church, occupier John Cherry, Marrick Church owning Low Bank House, occupier John Bousfield; Gilling Poor having land at 'Halfway House' (occ. Wm. Bell), Riddings (occ. Wm. Porter); Downholme Church at Riddings (E & H Woodward, occ.); Kirby Hill Church, near Ravensworth, having land, buildings, house at Castill (occ. Geo. Hird) and shooting rights Castill (occ. Bruce Ismay).

May the map on page 14 reproduced by the kind permission of the publisher of 'The Middleham Connection', Old School Arts Workshop, Middleham, provide you with some idea as to the power of Swaledale and Arkengarthdale's earlier land owners. May those who carry forth this heritage do so with the pride it so richly deserves.

**Panoramic view A Fremington (from Reeth)**

11

Plate 24: L/R Top (Kendall unless specified) - Ernest; Mary (m. Matt Calvert); Willie; Hilda; Annie Alderson; Ida; Willie Alderson; Jas.'s 2nd wife; Jn. Spensley; Hutchinson bros., Stubbing; Lizzie Ann; Eliz. Ruth Alderson; Francis Jas.; possib. Eliz. Alderson; unid.; Anna; Margaret Hannah; Nora Day; Miss Hird (m. Edwd. Pedley); Jas. himself; Percy; 4 unid. ch.; Harold Brown.

Plate 50: Top L/R: Billy Holland (underkeeper); Harold Brown; Henry Petty; Ted Hird; Bob Metcalfe; 3 standing- Underagent to Taylor, 'Buck' employee, Jas. Calvert; John Cherry; Kit Pratt; Norman Brown; Herbert Allan; Rbt. Croft; Neddy Allinson; Ben White; Jas. Calvert; Harry Calvert; Jack Metcalfe; Jack White; Thos. Wm. Brown; Matt Calvert; unid.; Ben Taylor (agent).

Plate 126: Back L/R: Mr. Shepherd (Headmaster); Alice Metcalfe ('Daggerstones'); Miss Siddal (teacher); Isabel Burton (Askrigg, Reeth); Mary Johnson (Ellerton); Lizzie Stoddart (High Row); Evelyn Johnson (Ellerton); Marjorie Cherry (Reeth); Nancy Woodmass (Reeth); Kathleen Barningham; Bessie Overend (Reeth); Evelyn Robinson (Reeth); Annie Petty; Alice Sunter ('Thirnswood'); Muriel Croft (Reeth); Rhoda Robinson (Reeth); Dora Appleton (Whitaside); Bessie White (Whitaside); Mattie Hammond ('Castle').

Plate 180: Reginald Place; W.C. Porter; Chas. Johnson; K. Barningham; Mark Alsop; Robt. Hammond; Cyril Barningham; Roy Postgate; Whitby Barningham; Arthur Johnson; Wm. Overend; Robin Pedley; Jn. Coates; Ronald Bowker; T. Arnold Hillary; Jas. Allison; Jn. Spence; Geo. Spence.

CONTINUED NEXT PAGE

\* LAY SUBSIDY ROLL 1301 (taxation for Scots campaigns and European military activities) includes Fremington: Jn. Sturdy, Nicholas of the Bank, Wm. of Fremington, Rbt. of Heggs, Thos. of the Bank, Simon Sudde, Rbt. Attebeck, Eudo of Castle, Rbt. son of Warin, Alan Belle; Grinton (including Harkerside and Whitaside): Wm. Overswale, Wm. the fuller, Thos. Frost, Jn. Fox, Peter Haudex, Stephen Collan, Henry Wode, Peter the Chaplain, Stephen of Haverdale, Jn. son of Eudo, Wm. Schakelock, Wm. Long, Roger son of Jn., Wm. the deacon, Jn. the blacksmith, Adam the carpenter, Paul the cobbler; others: Jn. of Gunnerside, Jn. son of the reeve, Rbt. of Ravenseat, Roger of Satron, Jordan of Kearton, Geoffrey of Ivelet, Stephen of the Wra, Sibil of Crackpot, Wm. of Blades, Thos. & Wm. of Mossdale, Simon of Oxnop, Wm. of Reeth, Thos. Underhou, Bernard del Banck, Wm. Bradrigg, Thos. del Dyke, Rbt. the cleric (Clarke), Geoffrey of Kearton, Rchd. Oysel, Simon Pegge, Rbt. son of Stephen, Wm. Godfrey, Lora the wife of Gilbert; and surnames of: Reeve, Ward, Miller, Milner, Weaver, Carter, Man, Pescodde, Todde, Kynge, Freeman, Praty, Shake, Dyl, Newetruite, Spirting, Blahat, Crobe, Tetty.

\* (As discussed in Edmund Cooper's Books and History of Richmond and Swaledale.)

Panoramic view B Fremington (from Reeth)

12

Plate 185: Top L/R: Jack Metcalfe; Jack Merry; Bob Hodge; Roland Woodward; Bob Hird; Mark Alsop; Bob Carter; Anthony Batty; Willie Alderson; Bertie Hutchinson; Jim Calvert; Whit Guy; Hind Hutchinson; Jim Pearson; Tom Longstaff; Tom Rutter; Sydney Hird; Jas. Allinson; Rev. Thomas; Ronnie Cherry; Vince Coates; Tom Batty; Jim Kendall; Bobby Rutter; Leonard Stones; Jas. Rutter; Jack Alderson; Bill Cherry; O.J. Kendall.

Plate 202: Top L/R: Jn. and Edwd. Cherry; unid.; Willie Alderson; Simon Cherry; John Reynoldson; Rev. Wendol Jones; Frank Pedley; Mary Jane Tebb; Rosie Allen; Mrs. Wm. Alderson (Robinson); Mrs. John Hillary; Canon Green's wife (Fothergill); Herbert Allan's sisters, Lily, Polly; Rhoda Hind; Mrs./Mr. Gott; Maud Cherry (Edwd's wife); Mary Jane Frankland; Jane (Cherry) Wendol Jones; Miss Allen; Doris, later Mrs. Tim Scratchard; Amy Dunn; baby unid.

Plate 232: Top L/R: Tom Hird; Tom Longstaff; Wesley Harker; Edwd. Stones; Elsie Metcalfe; Evelyn Hutchinson; Esme Binks; Mary Stubbs; Mary Peacock; Blanche Sowerby; Sheila Peacock; Betty Hird; Florence Hendry; Dennis Waller; Maurice Hutchinson; Ernest Binks; Leonard Stones; Geo. Thornborrow; Arnold and Sydney Hird; Jn. Stones; Stanley Waller; Arthur Shields; Thos. Harker; Jn. Stubbs; Willie Coates; Matty Harker; Margaret Hird; Mona Harker; Nancy Carter; Willie Stubbs; Willie Thornborrow; Ramsey Hutchinson.

Plate 286: Top L/R: Mr. Gott; Edwin Hillary; Mary Woodward; unid.; Mary Coates; Emma Longstaff; Manie Harker; Kathleen Hutchinson; Bessie Hird; Sarah Hannah and Geo. Scott; Ethel Carter; John and Sydney Hutchinson; Leonora Boyes; Olive Longstaff; Maggie and Mary Harker; Thora Carter; Raymond Longstaff; Jim Harker; unid; Fremie Hutchinson; Rbt. Hird; Bertie Hutchinson; Jas. Harker; Willie Carter; Jim Scott; Leo Hutchinson; Jimmy Hird; Jn. Rbt. Woodward; Kenneth Piercy; Charlie Wilson.

Plate 287: Back L/R: Jn. Scott (father); Margaret, Geo. Wm. (d. 1945,75) Harker; Herbert, Thomas Metcalfe; Alf Guy; Geo. Scott; Percy Metcalfe; Jas. (1899-1984), Geo. (1901-83) Harker; Ralph Scott; Jn. Metcalfe; Wm. (1906-88), Edith (1897-1903 m. Tom Highmoor, 'Park Head', Arkengarthdale) Harker; unid.; Eliz. (Scott, d.1955,79), Mary Eliz. (1902-45, m. Ernest Whitehead, later 'Park Head', Arkengarthdale), Ambrose (1903-81) Harker; Elizabeth Metcalfe.

Plate 290: L/R: Geo. Hird (C.B. Terrace Yard); Jn. Milner (above 'Cocker'); Tom Harker (Rigg Yard); Matthew Edwd. Stones (Seal Houses); Jn. Hird (The Mill); 'Janner'; Tom Coates (Eller's House); Betty Hird (The Mill); Mr., Mrs. Thos. Hind (blacksmith's); Ernest, Nellie Hird (High Green); Mrs. Jn. Milner; Mrs. Sarah Atkinson (Moor Intake); Mrs. Mary Ann Hird (Mill); Mrs. Hird (C.B. Terrace); Mrs. Templeton; Rhoda Hind; Geo., Hannah Harker (C.B. Terrace); Mrs. Thos. Harker; Mrs. Wm. Raine (Three Trees); Duke Hird; Blanche Dowson (Shaw).

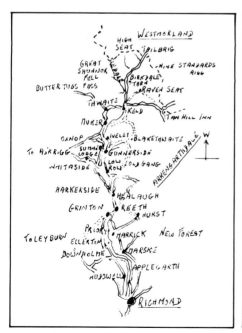

Plate 1: Swaledale.

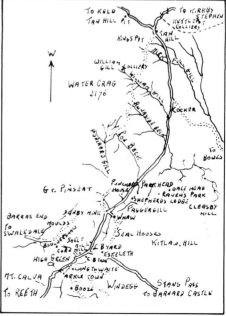

Plate 2: Arkengarthdale.

13

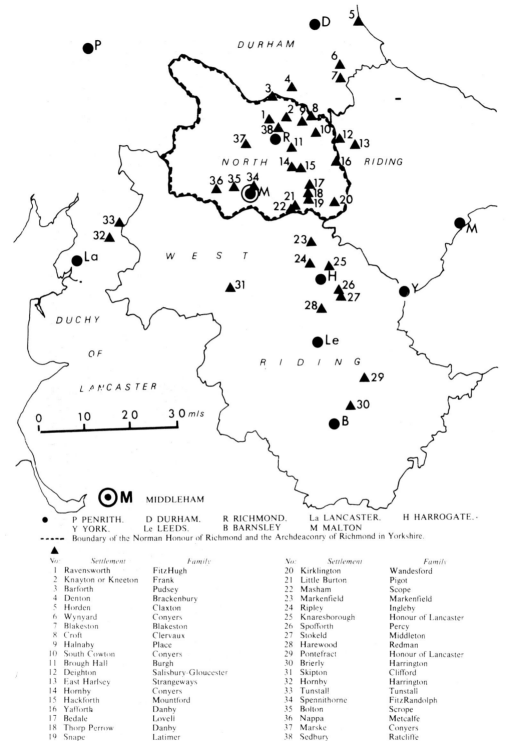

Plate 3: Map from 'The Middleham Connection' which details the exciting, historic links between Richard III in Wensleydale and Richmondshire (1471-85) and family names in this series.

| No: | Settlement | Family |
|---|---|---|
| 1 | Ravensworth | FitzHugh |
| 2 | Knayton or Kneeton | Frank |
| 3 | Barforth | Pudsey |
| 4 | Denton | Brackenbury |
| 5 | Horden | Claxton |
| 6 | Wynyard | Conyers |
| 7 | Blakeston | Blakeston |
| 8 | Croft | Clervaux |
| 9 | Halnaby | Place |
| 10 | South Cowton | Conyers |
| 11 | Brough Hall | Burgh |
| 12 | Deighton | Salisbury-Gloucester |
| 13 | East Harlsey | Strangeways |
| 14 | Hornby | Conyers |
| 15 | Hackforth | Mountford |
| 16 | Yafforth | Danby |
| 17 | Bedale | Lovell |
| 18 | Thorp Perrow | Danby |
| 19 | Snape | Latimer |
| 20 | Kirklington | Wandesford |
| 21 | Little Burton | Pigot |
| 22 | Masham | Scope |
| 23 | Markenfield | Markenfield |
| 24 | Ripley | Ingleby |
| 25 | Knaresborough | Honour of Lancaster |
| 26 | Spofforth | Percy |
| 27 | Stokeld | Middleton |
| 28 | Harewood | Redman |
| 29 | Pontefract | Honour of Lancaster |
| 30 | Brierly | Harrington |
| 31 | Skipton | Clifford |
| 32 | Hornby | Harrington |
| 33 | Tunstall | Tunstall |
| 34 | Spennithorne | FitzRandolph |
| 35 | Bolton | Scrope |
| 36 | Nappa | Metcalfe |
| 37 | Marske | Conyers |
| 38 | Sedbury | Ratcliffe |

● M MIDDLEHAM

● P PENRITH.  D DURHAM.  R RICHMOND.  La LANCASTER.  H HARROGATE.
  Y YORK.  Le LEEDS.  B BARNSLEY  M MALTON

- - - - Boundary of the Norman Honour of Richmond and the Archdeaconry of Richmond in Yorkshire.

▲

14

Plate 4: Very early photo of Healaugh, viewed across 'Stubbings Farm', Harkerside.

15

Plate 5: Healaugh from Reeth side, showing 'Manor House', 'Croft House', 'The Rookery' (1st 3L). 'Martin's Farm' opposite 'Croft House'. Approx. location of the Gaunt's Hall mid. R/.

Plates 6, 7, 8: 'Manor House', Healaugh, previous home of Places, from whom sons Frank Wesley (b. 1892), PLATE 8, of 'E. Windy Hall', Reeth, and Reginald Atkinson (b. 1896) descended of Jas. Ralph (b. 1866), Atkinson (b. 1823), Francis Place (m. Dorothy Atkinson of Arkengarthdale, 1819).

Plate 9: 1915. Descendants early Dolphin family L/R: Tamar Jane; Mary Ann; Anthony; Eliz; Evelyn; Annie Gertrude; Rhoda Hannah; Ernest; Margaret; Alice; father (Jn.); mother (Evelyn).

17

Plate 10: Hannah (Peacock) Place (b.1829), wife of Atkinson, family L/R: Sunter; Frank (m. Jane Martin); Dorothy (m. John Pedley); Geo. Rbt. All born 'Manor House', Healaugh. Not shown, Jn. (d. Windy Hall, Reeth), Jas. Ralph., Atkinson, Mary Anne (m. Jn. Martin).

Plate 11: Jane (Kendall) (b.1895), Reginald Atkinson, Stanley Francis (L/), Noel (R/) Place.

Plate 12: Grandmother and grandfather Raw with baby Jane Kendall.

Plate 13: L/R back - Frank ('Reels Head' brother to Thos. Hutchinson Kendall, Healaugh), Esther (Raw) Kendall; Thos. Raw Kendall, Mrs. Jane Place and Anne Kendall (bro/sisters); Henry Guy. Front L/R: Margaret Kendall; Margaret Guy; Margaret Esther Kendall, baby; Noel Place; Thos. Francis Kendall.

Plate 14: Stanley Place; Margaret, Thos. Francis, Annie (Brown) Kendall; Eliz. Brown; Henry Guy; Audrey Kendall.

Plate 15: Jane Kendall (1834-86, nee Hutchinson of Stubbings), wife of Mark, Low Whita (1832-1893). Mother to Francis (Reel's Head). Grandmother to Jane (Kendall) Place.

Plate 16: Thos. Hutchinson and 'Aunt' Bella. Is this Thomas of Stubbing (d.1899, 86), wife Isabella (d.1908, 89)?

Plate 17: Nancy Hillary, previously of Grinton. Grandmother to O.J. Kendall, Woodyard.

Plate 18: Ann Raw, aged 20, aunt to Jane (Kendall) Place.

20

Plate 19: Jn., Mary Ann (Place) and Jn. Thos. Martin, Healaugh. Dennis (gr. son), Margaret (gr. daughter) live Richmond.

Plate 20: c.1870. Francis Spensley Kendall (d.1901, Swale Hall, 91), 2nd wife, Margaret (Close). Parents of Mark (1835), Jas. (1840).

Plates 21, 22: Francis James Kendall (wife Nancy Hillary, father Jas., Swale Hall) and Frank Kendall. F.J.'s grandson, Alan, one of three current generation male Kendalls.

21

Plate 23: George (father), Cicily (mother), Francis, George, Mark, Susan, Fanny, Cissie, Annie Kendall.

Plate 24: Jas. Kendall, Swale Hall, far R/, mid. Row. 2nd wife a Metcalfe from Healaugh, 2nd from R/, top row. Names in text.

22

Plate 25: Archaeological dig, 1989, above Alex Alderson's bungalow, Healaugh. Richard Sunter, daughter, 'West House', far L/. Riddings to east.

Plate 26: Park Hall, Healaugh, to where Lord Wharton came. Previous holder of Manor, Sir Thomas Vachell, Coley, Reading, Berks.. Wm. the Conqueror's 4th son, Henry I, is buried in Reading Abbey.

Plate 27: Katie (Place) Cooper, son Edgar Arthur Cooper. Katie sister to Edgar and Evelyn Place, of parents Francis and Jane (Martin, b.1853), grandparents Atkinson (b.1823), Hannah (Peacock), all of Healaugh.

Plate 28: Cousins Muriel Robinson (parents below), Frank C. Place (of Edgar), toddler Cooper (see left).

Plate 29: c.1920's. Evelyn (Place), husband, Wm. Robinson, Park Hall Lane.

24

Plate 30: Elm Close, Healaugh, built below W. Riddings by Evelyn Robinson. Edgar Place lived here latterly.

Plate 31: Francis E. Place (b. 'Manor House' 1855-1944), aged 90.

Plate 32: Francis Callow Place, family, friends, W. Riddings, 1961.

Plate 33: Frank C., mother Jessey (Callow) Place.

Plate 34: Frank C. Place, W. Riddings, 1961, overlooking Harkerside. W. Riddings' substantial stone gate is on main roadside, west of Elm Close.

Plate 35: Frank C. Place, parents' Ariel car, 1924.

Plate 36: Jas. Callow, Jessey's father. Taught art, music to children of Hon. Lord Dundas at Aske Hall. F.E. Place, son-in-law (L).

Plate 37: The Callow home, Crakehall.

Plate 38: Francis C., father, Francis E. Place, 1931, namesakes of early Dales' Places 400 years ago, including Stanley F. (b.1925), son Francis Place (maternal gt. gr. fthr. Wm. Fothergill, master mason for Nunnington Hall Estate).

Plate 39: Jessey Place.

Plate 40: Wm. C. Porter (Wm. Sr's. son), son Jas., Riddings Farm, Healaugh. Plate 41: Wm. Porter, Sr., Riddings, ch.: Jn., Jas., Gregson, Emil, Len. Plate 42: 'Nannie' Johnny Pedley, 'West House', Healaugh. Plate 43: Norman, Mary Hillary (Reeth). Parents Mark, Betty (Hird, 'The Mill', Arkengarthdale). Plate 44: Margaret (Kendall) Hillary Place, sons Mark Hannam and Jn. Thos. Hillary. Plate 45: Sister to John Alderson ('Windy Hall'). Plate 46: Jas. Kendall's 2nd wife (her sister m. Jn. Alsop, Mark's father). Plate 47: Mrs. Hannah Salkeld (3 Bell sisters m. Salkeld, Curry, Porter), neighbour young Jn. Curry.

Plate 48: Honeymoon from 'Riddings' L/R: Emily Curry; Minnie (Alsop) Brown; Mary Hilda (Brown) Weighill; Margaret Alice Jackson; Francis Norman Brown (groom); W. Porter Sr.; Roland Weighill; Freda (bride); Maurice Porter.

Plate 49: 1920's Reeth Show. Thos. Wm. Brown (of 'Scar House'), father to above Browns.

29

Plate 50: Charlesworth and Metcalfe Tenants at Buck Hotel, Reeth. Names in text.

Plate 51: Jn. Jas., Geo. Emil, Freda, Maurice Bousfield, Gregson Bell, Wm. Campbell, Wm. Leonard, Annie, William Porter, Sr., Riddings.

Plate 52: Mary (d.1943, 61), Thos., Norman, Jn. Sunter (d.1958, 80), Riddings.

Plate 53: Simon Allen, Wm. Porter, Sr., Thos., Jn., Norman Sunter. Thos. m. Phyllis Clarkson (dtr. Sylvia m. Raymond Hunter, established Kearton Guest House, Thwaite).

Plate 54: Norman Sunter (b. 'Riddings' 1910), of 'Manor House', Healaugh. Shifting stones below 'Huttons Garth' (along main road). Riddings rises above road.

Plate 55: Norman's parents Jn., Mary (Alderson, dtr. Thos. Sr., Birk Park) Sunter at Spring End, near Gunnerside.

Plate 56: Jn. Sunter at Riddings. Son Norman lived 'Manor House' 45 years after marrying Vera 1945.

Plate 57: Jn. Mark, Richard Sunter, 'West House', Healaugh, opposite end village to 'Manor House' of parents'.

Plate 58: Hay time picnic, 'Manor House'. (R) Vera, Norman next to Malcolm Sunter ('Ash Dene', Low Whita, Brian's son, Whitaside). Malcolm m. Susan Highmoor, Park Head, Arkengarthdale.

Plate 59: Richard, Norman Sunter.

Plate 60: Presentation ceremony, Healaugh, for tidiest village.

Plate 61: Mark, Jn., Katy Sunter ('West House'), aunt Mary ('Birk Park'), whose early Reeth Young Farmers' training is put into practice daily on family farm. One of Mary's sons, Simon, is gamekeeper, Nidderdale, for Sir Joseph Nickerson Estate.

Plate 62: Margaret ('Park Hall'), father-in-law Alex Alderson ('Park Holme' 23 yrs., 'Park Hall' 27 yrs. with parents, there since c.1933, Wm., Margaret Alderson-Alex's maternal gr. parents Geo., Elizabeth, there from c. 1900 - John Martin before).

Plate 63: Sydney ('Park Hall' since c.'67), Margaret, Alex Alderson clipping sheep. 'Park Hall' across road from 'Birk Park'. Margaret's parents Henry Metcalfe Pedley, Eliz. (nee Sunter, Spring End).

Plate 64: L/R: Colin Hird (Crackpot); Alex, Mary, Dennis, Margaret, Sydney and Margaret (Pedley) Alderson; Margaret Mudd; Maureen, Henry, Wm. Spensley; Eliz. Pedley.

Plate 65: Sydney Alderson with £5000 tup. Paternal gr. fthr., Wm., born 'Shaw Farm', Arkengarthdale. 'Manor House' (32 acres) descended through Sydney's mother's (Mary) father's (Wm. of Hill Top, Arkengarthdale) uncle Enoch Atkinson.

Plate 66: Sydney, Mary, Margaret, Carol (m. Stephen Porter, Gregson's grandson, 'Crow Trees' Gunnerside, soon to Low Oxnop), Gillian, Alex Alderson.

Plate 67: Gillian (m. Kenneth Whitehead, 'Thwaite Farm', Muker), living in same house where ancestor four generations previous was born, Carol Alderson.

Plate 68: Margaret, Sydney, Gillian, born, Carol Alderson, beneath original 'Park Hall' door lintel inscribed LORD TW 1700.

37

Plate 69: From the walls of 'Birk Park' during the time of Thos. Alderson Sr. Possibly previous generation Aldersons (both pages).

Plates 70, 71 72: From above collection. Ident. welcome all. Book I provides excellent background for this family, as indeed applies for the whole of Book II.

38

**Plates 73, 74, 75, 76:** Thos. Alderson's granddaughter, Jenny Alderson Spensley Sunter, was born at 'Ivy Cottage', Healaugh, prior to her gamekeeper father being sent to Whaw.

39

**Plate 77: From collection of Elizabeth Ruth Alderson (b.1873), 'Windy Hall', Reeth, m. Thos. Wm. Brown (b.1873), 'Scar House', Reeth. Mother Eliz. Kendall, of Jas., 'Swale Hall'. Ident. welcome.**

**Plates 78, 79, 80: Collection of Thos. Alderson, Sr., 'Birk Park', Ident. welcome.**

Plate 81: Norman Sunter (R) at Salkeld's Cottages. 'Slack House' behind, 'Lock Heather' back (L). Between these two, not visible, are cottages of Gladys, John Hutchinson, and 'Ivy Cottage'.

Plate 82: Annie (Bell, of Wm., Healaugh), Maurice Porter, children Leonard, Emil, Jas.. Wm. Bell previous resident of 'Salkeld's cottages'.

Plate 83: 'Croft House' (adjacent 'Manor House'), Healaugh. Margaret Metcalfe, daughters, gr. child.

Plate 84: Pre-1900 'Lock Heather', below 'Hall Garth'. L/R: a Sunter, Margaret and Jn. Metcalfe, Mary Jane Tebb. Geo. Metcalfe said to have lived here. 1910 valuations show Thos. Sunter occupying house owned by Geo. Metcalfe's heirs, Thos. Metcalfe with substantial land, house of Matthew Whitelock's at 'Daggerstones'.

Plate 85: Jn. Metcalfe (1837-1913), gt.gr.fthr. of Jean (Tebb) Marr ('Long House', Low Row). Jean's grandfather was Rbt. Wm. Tebb (d.1898,35), Hurworth Place, Croft.

Plate 86: Early photo 'Croft House', 2nd house to left, entering Healaugh from Reeth.

43

Plate 87: Haytime at John Metcalfe's. Father-in-law, Geo. Metcalfe (1820-1894) m. Mary 1843 (d.1851), had daughter Margaret (d.1915), son Jn. (b. 1847). Geo's 2nd wife was Annas (d.1895, 81); brothers/sisters: Jas. (1805); Thos. (1807); Mary (1810); Jane (1812); Wm. (1815); Jn. (1817); Hannah (1822); Margaret (1826).

Plate 88: Jn., Margaret Metcalfe, 'Croft House' (showing possible early chapel window, now gone, extension to right).

Plate 89: 'Grandma' Mary Jane Tebb at 'Aunty' Janie Pedley's farm yard ('Crow Trees', Healaugh). Geo. Metcalfe's diary mentions niece Margaret Pedley, nephews Geo., Jn. Peacock, Thos. Metcalfe, sons Thos. B. Raw, John Metcalfe (living London with wife, Alis).

Plate 90: c.1899. Jn., Margaret Metcalfe, Mary Jane, Jn. Rbt. Tebb. (Jean Marr's father).

Plate 91: Unidentified woman at 'Crow Trees', a Pedley home. Another Healaugh Pedley, Wm. (d.1870, 72), had wife, Ann (d.1871), dtr., Isabella (d. 1861), grandson, Wm., son of a Thos.. 'Harker View' had a Wm. and Thos.

Plate 92: Mary Jane Tebb, Gladys Peacock, visiting 'Crow Trees'.

46

Plate 93: Jn., Margaret Metcalfe.

Plate 94: Jean (Tebb) Marr, Lawrence Barker ('The Rookery', descended of 400 years of Barkers, from Derbyshire, Lord Wharton's agents).

Plate 95: Jack White, working at 'Crow Trees'.

Plate 96: c.1931. Top L/R: Mary Jane Tebb; Miss and Mrs. Nattrass; baby Jean Tebb. Other Nattrasses, Healaugh: Jn. (d.1882, 69), wf. Isabella (d.1885, 74), son Metcalfe (d.1889, 47); Adam (d.1910, 58) ('Bank House'), wf. Margaret (d.1890, 39).

47

Plate 97: Geo., Janie, Thos. Pedley, 'Crow Trees'. Other Healaugh Pedley's- Metcalfe Pedley (1815-59), sons Henry (1848-69), Jn. (d.1888, 43).

.Plate 98: Thos., Geo. Pedley at Haytime, showing one of the dangers of hill farming, as Geo. prevents Thomas from toppling over.

48

Plate 99: Geo., Janie, Thos. Pedley with Jas. Dixon, Mary Jane Tebb, far right. Remaining unid.

Plate 100: 'Sunny Brae' (left), Mrs. Andrew Barningham's Healaugh P.O. Andrews gr.fthr., Mark Kendall (b.1886) previously 'West House', 'Swale View'. Thos. Hutchinson Kendall (1862-1943), lived 'Slack House'. R: 'The Nook', 'The Forge' (prev. included 'The Grove'), leading to Wm. Bell's and Fred Salkeld's cottages.

Plate 101: Simpsons (Blades, Healaugh, Low Row). Top L/R: Jas. (also father to Jas.); Maggie; Mary; Matt; Katie; Ida; Jas; Jane Eliz.; Nellie; Fred; Jn.; Jane Eliz. (Hazel); Annie. Cyril, Andrew Barningham farm 'Simpson's Land', Blades, also.

Plate 102: Angela (dtr), Andrew Barningham, son of Cyril ('Martins Farm', Healaugh). Maternal gr. parents: Mark, Jane Sunter, Whitaside. Maternal gt. gr. parents: Thos. Hutchinson Kendall, Jane Ann (Hammond).

Plate 103: Maurice Bousfield Porter, 'Riddings'. Officer many years 'Reeth Show', 'Reeth Young Farmers'. Wife Elsie (Hird).

Plate 104: Reeth Young Farmers, including Mary Sunter, Raymond Alderson, already featured in this series.

50

Plate 105: 'Sunny Brae', where Andrew (son of Cyril and May), wife Eileen, daughter Angela live.

Plate 106: Bob Metcalfe above Healaugh. Parents m. 1881, Wm. Jas. (b.1849, Gunnerside), Alice Hannah (Longstaff) (d.1884 birth of Rbt.).

Plate 107: L/R: William Alderson; Howard; sister Alice Metcalfe.

Plate 108: Howard Metcalfe, 'Daggerstones'. Maternal uncle/aunt Jn. Wm., Mary (Howard) Longstaff. Paternal uncle/aunt Wm., Annie (Metcalfe) Eggleston.

Plate 109: Healaugh, Salkeld's cottages (prev. Wm. Bell's), 'The Forge', 'The Grove', 'The Nook', home of Robert, Clara (Howard) Metcalfe.

Plate 110: John Curry (parents Wm., Emily (Bell)), outside Salkeld's store.

Plate 111: Clara Metcalfe, mother of Alice, Howard (resides 'Daggerstones', occupied 1910 by Thos. Metcalfe, owner Matthew Whitelock, Cogden Hall).

Plate 112: Bob Metcalfe (R), William Alderson (L) of 'Daggerstones'. Wm. brother to gamekeeper Mark, Low Row.

Plate 113: Wife of 'Nannie' Johnny Pedley (lived 'West House', Healaugh), carrying milk across road. Dorothy Place (b.1850/1) m. one of the Johnny Pedleys, had ch. Metcalfe, Hannah, Annie.

Plate 114: Bob Metcalfe, in front of 'Slack House' (Slacks early residents).

Plate 115: L/R: Albert Scott, uncle to Martha (Peacock) Morton, Arkengarthdale, and Bob Metcalfe. Albert's sister, Ellen Ann, m. Jas. Wm. Longstaff ('Raw Bank'), whose sister, Alice Hannah, was Bob's mother.

53

Plate 116: L/R: Bob Metcalfe; visitor; Mrs. Jn. Thomas Martin; visitor; Hannah Pedley (aunt to Margaret (Pedley) Alderson, 'Park Hall'); Dennis Martin.

Plate 117: Jas. Sunter (nephew to Thos. Alderson Sr., 'Birk Park'), gamekeeper at 'Thirnswood Hall' Healaugh, wife, Mary (Liddle, Arkengarthdale), daughters.

Plate 118: Fannie (dtr. of Jas. Place, 'Thierns'), Jas. (farmer later Fremington Mill), Dick Allinson, Cringley Hall, near Surrender Smelting Mill, Kearton Pasture, and Healaugh.

Plate119: Clara Metcalfe, daughter Alice, Arkletown, prior to living Healaugh.

Plate 120: John Alsop (b.1833), carrier, of Healaugh (parents Thomas (Hurst 1801-63), Eliz. (Dolphin, Marrick 1801-c.94). Wife Isabella (Metcalfe, sister m. Jas. Kendall, 'Swale Hall'), daughter Minnie (m. Thos. Harold Brown, now 92, one of Swaledale's oldest male residents).

Plate 121: Entrance to Reeth, via Silver Street, from Healaugh and upper Swaledale.

Plate 122: Silver Street, East End, and the Buck Hotel opposite the Burgoyne Hotel (originally Hill House, begun 1783 on Hatterbancks Close, Matthew Alderson's). Buck Hotel owner/occupier 1910, Ann Alderson. Geo. Garbutt there prev. and Pedleys among last locals.

Plate 123: L/R Top: Unid.; Tom Gill; Mark Alsop; Rbt. Hird; unid.; Rev. Thomas; Jack Merry.

Plate 124: c.1895, after leaving 'Castle'. Mark Alsop (1842-1902, farmer, butcher), wife, Margaret (Storey, Castle Bolton), Isabel. Mark son of Thos. (Hurst miner, farmer Castle), Eliz. (Dolphin, of Thos. Healaugh).

Plate 125: Dorothy Anne (Hammond, b.1865), Adam Geo. Barker's wife. Their ch. Jane, Eleanor, Jn., Geo., Adam, Alfred. Hammond family legend relates they were herdsmen of Wm. the Conqueror.

Plate 126: Reeth Friends School Housewifery Class. Names in text.

Plate 127: 'Lane House' (Reeth), Hammond and Place home. Wake Hammond (1836-1913), dtr. Jane Ann (b.1876) who married Geo. Calvert, 'Laykin', Low Row. Wake's wife Sarah Pedley (1839-1907, Healaugh). Ch. born Riddings: Adam Edwd. (1869); Edwd (1871); Thos. (1873).

58

Plate 128: L/R: Sarah Ann (Bousfield); Adam; Jane Ann; Sarah, Wake Hammond; Betty, Tom, possibly another Woodward; Thomas Hammond; Mary Eliz. Woodward; baby Albert, Edwd. Hammond; Mary Margaret Woodward; 2 unid.

Plate 129: 'Arkle House' (past home Jn. Blenkiron), nr. Reeth Mill. Here above married couple supported 'Ned's' carrier business, looking after Uncle Thos. Pedley, Sarah's brother, when could no longer care for himself in the Healaugh family home.

Plate 130: Back: Wm. Hammond; Maggie, Jimmy Harker; a friend; Ned Hammond; Betty Woodward; Geo. Harker; Betty (Hammond, dtr. to Ned, Mary Margaret).

Plate 131: 1980. Wm. (b.1908), Martha (Hammond, b.1909) Moralee, Marjorie (Peacock), Albert (b.1902) Hammond, Martha's brother. At Castle, where Albert lived 1918-53, moving into Congregational Chapel's Manse Cottage (Chapel caretakers 31 yrs.).

**Plate 132:** Edwd. (b.Rawcroft), Matty Hird outside Rawcroft (where lived until 1960, then 'Dikehouse', Harkerside (7yrs.), 'Rookby Scarth', where Matty still lives with son, Lawrence, wife Elsie and family).

**Plate 133:** Edwd., Matty (Templeton) Hird, 1949. Matty's parents lived 'Greenhouse', Hurst (1915), 'Heggs', Reeth (1922), 'Turnip House', nr.Smarber (from 1940's).

**Plate 134:** Lawrence, husband to Elsie (Milner, Gunnerside), grandson of Edwd. ('Sturfitt Hall', Marrick Parks - 1922, Rawcroft - 1937, Mill Hill, Reeth - 1938, Arkle Town - 1950), Mary (Alderson, 'Castle') Hird, with mother.

Plate 135: Geo. Templeton (b.c.1842), champion sheepclipper, 1st Templeton at Rawcroft. Ch. : Jane (m. Thos. Alcock, Cringley); Jn.; Thos. (m. Margaret Eliz. Hayken); Agnes (m. a Wilkinson): Geo. (unmarried d. Rawcroft.).

Plate 136: L/R: Douglas; Mary; Thos.; Margaret Eliz. Templeton (m.1914). Other ch. Matty, Ida, Stanley.

Plate 137: Rawcroft, the back. 1600's, 1700's home for Hutchinsons, Clarksons, Coates.

Plate 138: Mary (Alderson) Hird's mother, of 'Castle', maternal gr.mthr. to Edwd., husband of Matty. Edwd.'s father, grandfather also Edwd. of 'Sturfitt Hall'.

Plate 139: Cousins (via Geo. of Smarber) of Edwd. Hird (Matty's husband), Ernest (m.Mary Appleton, Whitaside), Jn. Edwd. (b.1904, 'Castle', m. Rose Brown, Haverdell). Their brother Geo. m.Belle Coates, now Crackpot.

Plate 140: 'Castle', near 'Sturfitt', past home for Hammonds (pre-Conquest name Fitz-Hammon), Aldersons, Hirds. 1600's, 1700's, Galloway, Hillary, Liddle, Hall, Hardcastell, Atkinson, Spence, Cherry, Tennant, Chapman.

Plate 141: District Council Members' Proclamation of H.M. Queen Elizabeth II, 1952. L/R: Rbt. Carter; Edwd. Pedley; Oliver Stones; Edwd. Kearton; Tim Raw; Mr. Nixon; Malcolm Scott; J.F.H. Kendall; Jas. Coates; Clarkson Jackson; Thos. Brown.

Plate 142: John Clarkson (b.1897), Margaret Alice (Brown) Jackson (b.1899), Thelma, Mary, Jn. Keith. Continued Jn. Jackson's (b.1858) Silver Street business until sale 1965.

Plate 143: Matty Moralee at Castle, descended of Adam Edwd. (1869), Wake (1836), Edwd. (1809), Thos., Geo. (1737, Fremington), Rchd. (Frem.), Symond (1658), Rchd. (m.Sith Hutchinson, 1640).

Plate 144: Reeth Show 1957. L/R: Dr. W.C. Speirs; J.F.H. Kendall; Mrs. G.I. Barker; A.A. Scarr; G.I. Barker; Lady Sopwith; R.W. Wilson; Sir T.O.M. Sopwith, O.B.E.; A.J.E. Durston; B.T. Hart.

Plate 145: Reeth Show, 1906. Substantial properties background 'Grinton Lodge', 'Swale Hall'.

Plate 146: Edwd. and Mary (Alderson) Hird at Marrick Parks, originally at 'Sturfitt Hall', homes 1600's, 1700's for Thomas Wharton, Aldersons, Robinsons, Clarksons, Haykin, Wholey, Hillary, Dolphin, Brown, Harker, Wensley, White.

Plate 147: Mrs. Jn. Hillary, 'Windy Hall', Reeth, c.1930. Jn's brother Mark, inherited Reeth shop after Jas. R. Place's (stepfather) death.

Plate 148: Rbt. Wm. Weighill (b.1882), wife Mary Hilda (b.1896 of Thos. Wm., Eliz. Ruth Brown). Rbt. descended of Rbt. (Reeth, Crook), Wm. (Spennithorne, Reeth Mill), Christopher and Ann (Greathead) (Spennithorne), Wm. and D. (I'anson), (E. Whitton, m.1767).

Plate 149: From Eliz. Ruth (Alderson) Brown's photo album.

66

Plate 150: Wilson White, Jn., Mark Hillary, ch. of Thos. Hannam and Margaret (Kendall) Hillary.

Plate 151: Frank Kendall (Sorell Sykes), to N.Z. with sister Eliz., cousin Geo. (Swale Hall), who married Eliz.

Plate 152: Reginald Atkinson Place, Jn. & Mark Hillary's half brother. Head teacher Reeth Friends School c.1926/7 for 30 years.

Plate 153: Eliz. (Kendall) Alderson, Jn.'s wife ('Windy Hall'), sister-in-law to Joby Alderson, 'New House', Arkengarthdale. Mother of Jas., Wm., Eliz. Ruth; Annie; Margaret (m. Thos. Raw, Marrick).

Plate 154: L/R: Mary Ann (Thwaites) Kendall (maternal gr.mthr. to Reginald Atkinson Place), Nanny (Allen) and Wm. Thwaites. Mary Ann sister to Wm., Adam Thwaites, co-heirs to Jas. Pratt's Dubuque, Iowa estate, $60-$80,000 U.S.

Plate 155: Mark Kendall (b.1835), Mary Ann's husband, father to Margaret (b.1861).

Plate 156: Margaret Kendall, wife of (1) Thos. Hannam Hillary (2) J.R. Place (b.1866).

Plate 157: Grandfather Thwaites. Photo taken Dubuque, Iowa.

68

Plate 158: Possibly Margaret Kendall (R), mother (L).

Plate 159: From Eliz. Ruth (Alderson) Kendall's album.

Plate 160: Believed to be Thos. Hannam Hillary. A Thos. Hannam Hillary d.1889 (b.1863), mother Jane (1824-99, Grinton).

Plate 161: From Eliz. Ruth's album, containing many Kendalls, Aldersons & Browns.

Plate 162: Probably Wm. Kendall (d.1952, 69), family. Wm. of 'Swale Hall', member Reeth Brass Band, Grinton Choir, old boy of Fremington Church of England Endowed School.

Plate 163: Top L/R: Annie Alderson; Mary Hilda Brown (Thos. Wm.'s dtr); Thos. Raw ('The Lodge', Marrick); wife Margaret (below); Bessie; Annie.

Plate 164: 'Windy Hall', Reeth. Front L/R: Eliz. (Kendall); Annie (b.1873); Margaret; Eliz. Ruth (b.1873) Alderson. Jn., sons Jas., Wm. to rear among others.

Plate 165: Francis Norman Brown, 'Scar House', Reeth (m.Freda Porter, 'Riddings'), of Thos. Wm., Eliz. Ruth Brown.

Plate 166: Eliz. Ruth, Annie Alderson (twins), 'Windy Hall'.

Plate 167: Believed to be Harkers (lady possibly Place). Reader ident. welcome.

Plates 168, 169: The changing face of High Row, Reeth. First of three successive views. L/R: 1st doorway left, Thwaites' Drapers, late 1800's; Victoria House; Kings Arms Hotel (landlady Mary Jane Peacock in first two); James Place's Store; Geo. Barningham's clog shop late 1800's; Postgate's Stores; Dr. Speirs' surgery; The Buck Hotel; Burgoyne Hotel opposite.

**Plate 170:** Note Victoria House no longer a guest house and Pedley's Boot Stores has appeared, with cafe between the Place and Postgate Stores.

**Plate 171:** c.1920. Ryder & Nix's 'Heather Cafe' in place of earlier and what looks like a bank's sign.

**Plate 172:** Fred, William Peacock, Kings Arms Hotel, Reeth 1909. Mary Jane Peacock bought 'The Laurels' before she died, leaving Nellie Elwood, housekeeper to the boys there.

Plate 173: Willie, Mary Jane Peacock's son, who moved with boys and Nellie Elwood to The Laurels after 'Kings Arms' sale.

Plate 174: Willie Peacock, 'Raikes Cottage, Nellie Elwood, who later bought it and bequeathed it to her niece, Sylvia (Cleminson) Durston.

Plate 175: Joined view of Reeth L/R from 'The White Stores' of Margaret and Mary Hodgson (possibly inherited from Wm. Hodgson early 1900's) to present day Barclays Bank at 'Hudson House'. See PLATE 278 for missing middle view.

Plate 176: Reeth Friends Schoolboys. Top L/R: Alfred Kendall; Jn. Franklin; Oliver Blenkiron; Rchd. Moore; Tom Pedley; Edwin Moore; Roland Swales; Headmaster J.W. Moore; Jn. Dunn; Reginald Place (headmaster later); Roland Allen; Horn Peacock; Harold Brown; Harold Blenkiron; Clarkson Jackson.

Plate 177: Reeth shelter, local 'Parliament'. L/R: Maurice Porter; Fremie Hutchinson; Joe Sunter; Ernest Dolphin; visitor; Wm. Harker.

Plate 178: Robert ('Jackie') Cleminson, Sylvia Durston's father, 'Cosy Cottage', Reeth. Rbt.'s sister, Lizzie, m.Thos. Richardson, whose daughter, Gladys Gill, family feature Book I.

Plate 179: Reeth Show 1906. Now held August bank holiday each year in fields by 'The Woodyard'.

**Plate 180: Reeth School Boys, Reginald Place, Headmaster. See text for names.**

**Plate 181: Awarding of the combined Dales' Sports plaque, begun c.1924.**

77

Plate 182: 'Burgoyne Hotel', Reeth Green, with 'The White House' in hills beyond on Fremington Edge.

Plate 183: Reeth 'Rascals Concert Party' outside Burgoyne Hotel. L/R: Tim, Doris Scratchard; Oliver Blenkiron; Tom Milner (singing); Dick Peacock; Jim Kendall; Geo. L. Barker.

78

Plate 184: A. Scarr (Barclays Bank Mgr.); Dick Lawson; Fred Hope Wilson (long-serving Pres., Reeth Show); Hubert Horn ('Sorrel Sykes'); Margaret, gr.fthr Lawson.

Plate 185: Swaledale Mixed Band at the Burgoyne. Names in text.

Plate 186: The Friends School Reeth, 1936. Reginald Place, Headmaster 30 years. from c.1926/7.

Plate 187: Earlier photo, Arthur Shepherd, Headmaster until he left c.1926/7 to be the Labour M.P. for Darlington.

Plate 188: The Clarksons, top L/R: Bessie; Jn. (b.1858, father Jas. b.1824); Alice (of Jas., Eliz. Brothers/sisters: Mary; Mahala; Woodward; Woodward; Kearton; Jas; Sunter; Jn.); Mary; Jas; Jn. Clarkson Jackson (m. Alice, sister to Harold Brown).

Plate 189: L/R: prev. Lily Dixon; Alice Clarkson (sister to Marmaduke, Vet, Satron); Miss Spensley (Robin Gate, Feetham); Alice Jackson; unid.; Mrs. Edwd. Hammond (dtr. Eliz. m.Geo. Harker); unid.; Mark Alsop, Jn's son, Harold Brown's father-in-law.

Plate 190: Reeth Band. See Page 44, Book I for members. Photo earlier ident. as Low Row's band.

Plate 191: Reeth Football Team. Top L/R: Jn. Dunn; Jim Kendall; Sydney Coates; Leslie Barningham; Robin Pedley; Willie Pedley; Percy Cleminson; Howard Metcalfe; Newton Whitehead; Arnold Hillary; Simon Cherry; Cyril Barningham; Rbt. Hammond; Leslie Bainbridge.

Plate 192/3: Peat Gate Hill, rising from Feetham. Thos. Wiseman, PLATE 193, one of the last Wisemans to live over hilltop, 'Peat Gate Head'. See text for detail's of Queen Elizabeth I's extensive land sale to Richard Wiseman, 1599.

Plate 194: Swaledale Home Guard. Reader ident. requested.

Plate 195: Reeth Friends School, c.1920. Reader ident. requested.

Plate 196: 1922 Reeth Friends School, Woodworking Class. Reader ident. requested.

84

Plate 197: Reeth Friends School. Reader ident. requested. Established through an original trust funded by brothers Geo., Leonard Raw 1785/7, and John Raw in 1855, transferred from earlier location to current one, 1862.

Plate 198: c.1926/7. Showing off Dales' Sports Award for Reeth Friends School. Reader ident. requested.

Plate 199: The Friends School Reeth had 5 Headmasters to 1862. Raw Charity continued for educational purposes, but the North Riding Co. County Council's Education Committee bought Reeth School in 1939.

Plate 200: Reeth Football Club, top L/R: Wm. Porter; Geo. Merry; Howard Metcalfe; Geo. Spence; Sydney Coates; Jas. Kendall; Simon Cherry; unid.; Rbt. Hammond; Frank Pedley; unid.

Plate 201: Reeth Women's Institute Concert.

Plate 202: Reeth Congregational Prize Choir, c.1911. Names in text.

Plate 203: 'The Laurels', centre, 'The White Stores', right. Thos. Peacock, butcher employed by Healaugh's Martin family, had the corner properties on right bend of this road. Reeth Workhouse located behind these.

Plate 204: Reeth from above, with: Grinton, foreground; Fremington between two bridges and off photo to right; 'The Woodyard' behind 2nd bridge, middle left; Arkengarthdale Road middle back; road updale by Reeth School (the Porters' 'Riddings Farm' above).

Plate 205: Early photo Fremington. 'Draycott Hall' adjacent to 'A.D. House', hidden by bottom cluster of trees.

Plate 206: Henry, Grinton gamekeeper, Mary (Simpson) Petty at 'The Grange'. Grandparents to Harry, Alf, Mary (Calvert) Petty. This Simpson family lived 'Bird Nest', Blades.

Plate 207: Jas. Simpson (d.1949), brother to Mary (left). Simpsons are one of the earliest families in Swaledale.

Plate 208: 'A.D. House', Fremington home of the Cherry family. Buried in Low Row U.R.C. Chapel is Simon (d.1901, 64), wife Mary (d.1924, 80), dtr. Mary (d.1901, 30), son Jas. (d.1874).

Plate 209: Behind 'A.D. House'. L/R: Simon; Jane; father; mother; Edwd., wife Maud Eliz., Jn. (all sitting); Joseph (standing). Another brother, Wm Alderson Cherry, d. 1904, 24.

Plate 210: Edwd. Cherry (d. 1939, 69), J.P., Auctioneer, Secretary Reeth Congregational Chapel 42 yrs.

Plate 211: Edwd.'s mother of 'A.D. House', Fremington. Her husband Simon was agent of the Old Gang leadmines for 31 years until his death 1901, succeeding agent Francis Taylor. 14 years after this appointment, on Thos. Raw's death, Simon Cherry became agent to Sir. Francis E. Denys, 'Draycott Hall', holder of Swaledale mineral rights at that time.

Plate 212: Believed to be an early Simon Cherry and wife.

Plate 213: Joseph Cherry, 'A.D. House', Fremington.

Plate 214: John Cherry, 'A.D House', Fremington.

Plate 215: Believed to be Wm. Alderson Cherry, 'A.D. House'.

Plate 216: Joan (b. 1915), father Joseph and wife Margaret (b. 1892, parents Christopher, Margaret (Dixon) Easby of Winton), Frank Cherry (b. 1921), Joan's brother, Joseph's son).

Plate 217: Frank and Edward (b. 1918) Cherry, brothers. Among the 1600's Cherrys were Edwd., Geo., Jas., Rbt., and Thos. of Kearton, Blades, Feetham.

Plate 218: L/R: Rev. R. Wendol Jones (1876–1952); Margaret (Easby) Cherry; Gwen Wynne Jones; Jane (Cherry) Wendol Jones, previously 'A.D. House'.

Plate 219: The current generation Simon Cherry, a vet, of Bishop Burton, E. Riding.

Plate 220: Pamela, Lorna, Joseph, Edwd., twins Simon, Paul, Margaret, Barbara, Sandra Cherry.

Plate 221: Raw Bank, Arkle Town, Langthwaite, High Green and C.B. Hotel beyond. Plate 222: Inset, bottom right Plate 221 ....
Raw Bank. Alice Metcalfe, Mary (Howard), husband Jn. Wm. Longstaff (parents John, Mary Jane, nee Hutchinson, Yealands).

Plate 223: C.B. Hotel, 'Scarr House' with hillside farms in background.

Plate 224: Langthwaite, Arkengarthdale, set of numerous films and used for sequences in the Herriot series.

Plate 225: High Green, Arkengarthdale, across road from Langthwaite. Some past residents: Garbutts; Scotts; Jake Dobson (the larger front); Nellie, Ernest Hird (a shop); Tom, Nancy Carter (w/garden); Jack, Mary Ann Hird (also Sunday School, Literary Institute); Wesleyan Chapel.

Plate 226: Arkengarthdale views, L/R: 'Scarr House'; St. Mary's Church, Vicarage; High Green and Langthwaite; Langthwaite; bottom right viewing Raw Bank (front), Arkle Town, Langthwaite, High Green.

Plate 227: Arkle Town and beyond during snow. 'Calva View' and 'New House' (rear) closest to road.

Plate 228: 'Scarr House', Arkengarthdale, past home of the late Sir Thomas Sopwith.

Plate 229: The Stang Road from Arkengarthdale to Barnard Castle, where corn was taken to be ground for bread-baking and malting. 'Eskeleth Hall' to left.

Plate 230: 'Eskeleth Hall', built by the Jaques family.

Plate 231: Mary, Edie Watson, 'High Eskeleth', whose parents were Joseph and Mary, sister Barbara, brother Charles.

Plate 232: Arkengarthdale School's children at 'The Mill'. A later book will cover more of their families. Names in text.

Plate 233: Arkengarthdale Sunday School, top L/R: Hilda Atkinson; Mary Harker; Minnie, Willie Stones; Madge Metcalfe; Jonathan Atkinson; Geo. Scott; Annie, Jas. Harker; Jack Franklin; Jim Scott; Jack Atkinson.

99

Plate 234: Arkengarthdale's C.B. Terrace, Mills. The Barninghams had a family home at 'Hillside', above, and another along The Stang Road, which travelled over the bridge to Barnard Castle.

Plate 235: Wm. Longstaff Stones' bus from Arkengarthdale to Richmond.

Plate 236: c. 1920. William L. Stones, Martha (Peacock) Morton, Wm. Hird.

**Plate 237: Whaw.**

101

Plate 238: Nellie Stones, past resident of Whaw, 'New House' Arkletown (from age 4), 'White House' (across the road from Arkle Town), currently of 'Arkle Barn' Arkle Town.

Plate 239: Matthew Edwd. Stones (b. 1863), Nellie's gr.fther., son of Edwd. (1820-83), Dinah (Tilburn) Stones.

Plate 240: Famed water diviner, Matthew Edwd. Stones, whose wife was Alice Longstaff, parents to Wm. Longstaff Stones, Oliver, Geo., Minnie, Nellie.

Plate 241: 'The Rigg' (below 'Cocker House'), past home Ralph Harker, the Dobsons, later Nellie (Peacock) Hird (Ralph Wharton Hird's wife and Martha's sister).

Plate 242: Martha (Peacock) Morton, outside 'Cocker House', said to be part of Eliz. I's gift to Thos. Peacock for war assistance. Legend relates that Punchard, Seal Houses, Shaw Farms and Spanham (over The Stang) were separate in Arkengarthdale Manor sales.

Plate 243: Jas., Violet Hird ('Cocker' Jn.'s parents), Martha, (Violet's sister), Tom Hird (Nellie, Ralph Wharton Hird's son).

Plate 244: Mrs. Thos. (Emily Ann Scott) Peacock, Tom, Nellie, Martha at Whaw, next door to Martha, Wm. Caygill.

Plate 245: Isabella (Ralph Caygill's wife), brother-in-law Wm. Caygill, Ralph's niece, Emily Ann Peacock.

Plate 246: Martha (Peacock) Morton, 8-10 yrs. old, living 'Cocker House' with nephew 'Cocker' Jn. Hird.

Plate 247: Jas. Hird, whose gr. parents were Rbt., Mary Ann (Whitehead) Hird, 'The Mill'. Rbt.'s ch.: Ralph Wharton (m. Nellie Peacock); Joseph (m. Phyllis Milner, 'Mill Intake'); Jack (Jas.'s fthr); Annie (m. Thos Peacock, Reeth butcher); Eliz. (m. Mark Hillary, Reeth); Nellie (m. Tom Gill, Reeth); Alice (m. Frank Coates, Marrick); Jas.; Thos.; Rbt; Sydney.

Plate 248: 'Cocker' Jn., Jas.'s son, whose smiling face is seen through the Dales delivering logs, driving coaches, taxis.

Plate 249: Mary Liddle (future wife Jas. Sunter, gamekeeper, 'Thirnswood Hall', Healaugh), Wm., Martha Caygill. Martha sister to Joe, Ann Spence, 'Feetham Farm'.

Plate 250: Fanny Caygill.

Plate 251: Grandmother Caygill (Mrs. Hannah Scott's mother).

Plate 252: Alf Caygill (d. aged 80), Wm.'s brother.

Plate 253: Alf Caygill. Brothers/sisters: Jn. Thos; Wm.; Ralph; Joseph; Dorothy Hannah (m. Jas. Scott, father of Ellen Ann, Emily Ann, Martha, Hannah, Wm., Tom, Alf, Albert, Jack, Ralph, Raymond).

Plate 254: Joseph Caygill and son.

Plate 255: Joseph Caygill's daughter, Lizzie (m. Thos. Atkinson, 'Moor Intake').

106

Plate 256: Wm. Raine, 'Three Trees', Arkengarthdale.    Plate 257: Sarah Raine, Wm.'s wife.

Plate 258: Mr. and Mrs. Thos. Harker, 'Yew Tree House', Arkengarthdale.

Plate 259: Ralph Harker, 'The Rigg'. Plate 260: Wm. (parents Jas., Hannah (Caygill)) Scott, son. Plate 261: Unid. Arkengarthdale woman. Plate 262: Mary, Wm. Scott. Plate263: Wm.'s sons Geo., Jim (m. Dora Appleton, 'Hollins Farm', Whitaside, farmed Hurst, 'Dale Head', Ark.). Plate 264: Mary, Hannah, Jack Scott. Plate 265: Joby Alderson, 'New House', Arkle Town, brother Jn., 'Windy Hall'. Plate 266: Reg. Raisbeck, sister Mary. Plate 267: Lawrence, Annie (Milner) Peacock.

Plate 268: Geo. Barningham, Reeth cobbler. Ch.: Plates 269/70/71/72/73/74. Plate 269: Jas. (b. 1884), Kenneth's father. Plate270: Geo. Wm. (b. 1878). Uncle/Aunt: Samuel, cobbler, 'Hillside', off Stang Road, Sarah (Stoddart) Barningham. Plate271: Ernest (b. 1885), son Cyril, farmer, Healaugh, Feetham. Plate 272: Tom Longstaff (b. 1891), moved to Croft. Plate 273: Rbt. Daykin (b. 1893). Plate274: and Emily Barningham (m. Thos. Alderson, Jr.). Plate 275: Alice Hannah (Longstaff) Metcalfe, Mary's sister (right). Plate 276: Mary (Longstaff), George Barningham's wife, Thos.'s granddaughter. Brother Jas. Wm. m. Ellen Ann Scott.

Plate 277: 1921. Arkengarthdale School. Reader ident. requested. Plate 278: Norman, Rchd. Sunter (Healaugh) cutting Reeth Green. Plate 279: Ernest Peacock, Lawrence's brother. Plate 280: Jn. Wm. Longstaff, Raw Bank, nephew to Hannah Longstaff, Bob Metcalfe's mother. Plate 281: c.1899, Jas. Metcalfe (b. 1866, Tan Hill) daughter Eliz., son. Sir Jas. Metcalfe, 'Nappa Hall', Wensleydale (related by marriage to Wm. Conyers, Marske) granted 1532 mining lease Honours of Richmond, Middleham, descended to Christopher Metcalfe 1544 another 21 yrs.. 1605, Sir Rbt. Stapleton, Sir Jn. Mallory held Arkengarthdale mines by Queen Eliz. I. Plate 282: Mary Kipling, Nellie Stones' maternal gr.mthr. Top L/R: Ada (Nellie's mother); Eliza; Eliz.; Winnie, Nellie. Plate 283: Nora (Metcalfe) Wagstaff, dtr. Jean, whose father had Arkengarthdale's Chert quarries. Plate 284: A Rucroft.

Plate 285: Arkengarthdale School, 25 Nov. 1909. Reader ident. requested.

Plate 286: Arkengarthdale School, 1921. Names in text.

Plate 287: Scott, Harker, Metcalfe family group. Names in text.

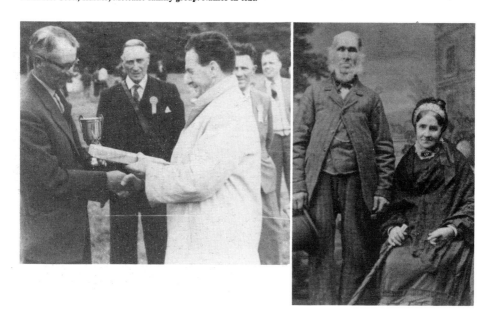

Plate 288: Arkengarthdale Sports, late 1960's. L/R: Wm. Harker ('Dale Head', 'Yealands'); Edwd. Hird (Rawcroft); Thos. Sunter ('Spring End', Gunnerside); Jn. Stones (Seal Houses).

Plate 289: Jas. Espiner Harker ('Scar House', Muker), 2nd wife (from Gunnerside). His brothers/sisters: Wm; Margaret; Jn.; Hannah. Parents Simon, Jane (Espiner).

Plate 290: Sewing Circle, Arkengarthdale. Names in text.

Plate 291: Rhoda Hind's 1925 Wedding to Wm. Hutchinson. Full reader ident. requested for future publication.

**Plate 292: Arkengarthdale Football Team. Top L/R: Fred Walmsley; Tom Barningham; Jn. Thos. Milner; Abraham Harker; Duke Hird; Wm. Stones; Mrs. Thomas Peacock; Raymond Longstaff; Tom Hird; Wm. Hird; Mary Milner; Tom Milner; Jas. Hird; Rbt. Hird.**

**Plate 293: Reader ident. requested this Arkengarthdale photo.**

Plate 294: Arkengarthdale Band 1907. Reader ident. requested.

Plate 295: Sunday School Outing Arkengarthdale. Reader ident. requested.

Plate 296: Early photo in the Stones family. Reader ident. requested.

Plate 297: Arkengarthdale Sports. Gentlemen L/R: Ralph Wharton Hird; Clifford Harker; Wesley Hird; Jim Carter; Lesley Harker; Wesley Harker; Arthur Barningham.

**Plate 298: 1907. Daughters Pratt, Margaret (Harker) Demain, Kearton, L/R: Eleanor (age 58, m. Jas. Alderson, Grinton); Ruth (68, m. Matthew Cherry); Alice (53); Barbara (64); Margaret (60, m. Joseph Hird, miner, widower, Arkengarthdale).**

**Plate 299: Thos. (1867-1927 b. Castle, left 1895 for Lancs.), Eliz. Ann (Harker 1873-1947, b. Low Row) Alsop. Ch.: Lily; Geo. Wesley; Margaret Ellen.**

Plate 300: Isaac Hillary (1835-1903, parents Joseph, Margaret). Wife Mary (Hall, 1846-93, High Green, Arkengarthdale). Her parents, David (1812-59, High Green), Maria (Leonard Coates' dtr. b. 1785).

Plate 301: Could be: David, Maria Hall; Michael, Mary Raisbeck; Jospeh, Margaret Hillary. David's sister, Nanny, m. a Wharton and d. 1834, Arras Close, Westmorland. Her sister Mary d. 1820, Wharlton.

Plate 302: c. 1900 Faggergill lead miners, L/R top: Ralph Harker; Pratt Demain; Ben Hall; Wm. Longstaff; Geo. Harker; Rbt. Hird; Ashton Stones; Jas. Waller; Mark Alsop; Jn. Ward; Rbt. Longstaff; Jack Alsop.

Plate 303: 1907. Wm., Charlotte, Ada, baby Chalder. Wm.'s gr.fthr., Matthew, left Arkengarthdale c. 1830 for Co. Durham.

Plate 304: Early 1900's. Edith Mary Pusey, Jemima Sarah (Chalder) Pusey's dtr., Matthew, Mary Chalder's gr. dtr.

Plate 305: Ronald Pusey Atkinson, Dorothy (Atkinson) Cluderay, Jemima Sarah Chalder's grandchildren.

Plate 306: Charlotte Chalder, family, after Wm. killed in Army, 1915.